CONTENTS

Post Punk Football	1
Introduction	3
Why is Our Game Like This?	9
Why Do Football Clubs Matter?	33
The Rise of Supporter Power	48
The Clubs	65
Lewes FC	66
AFC Wimbledon	73
Clapton CFC	80
FC United of Manchester	85
Bury AFC	92
Exeter City	98
The Fan Led Review	105
The Future	124
Books By This Author	153
Books By This Author	155

Books By This Author

POST PUNK FOOTBALL

JIM KEOGHAN

To Nicky. My Everything

INTRODUCTION

Back in 2014, I wrote *Punk Football,* my exploration of supporter activism and fan ownership in the English game. The book looked at the journey that fans had taken over the previous 25 years, a journey that had seen them become politicised like never before.

I remember finishing the book with a prediction, that 'Punk Football', as the fan ownership movement was sometimes called, was poised to make the next step, to move from the margins to the mainstream. It was a prediction based on the fact that, during the previous few decades, supporter ownership had gone from a rarity in the game to spread across it. It might have been more commonly seen in the lower reaches of the sport, specifically in the world of semi-professional football, but it nevertheless seemed to possess a sense of irresistible momentum. Along with gaining a decent foothold in non-league football, fan-owned clubs, in the guise of AFC Wimbledon, Exeter City and Wycombe Wanderers had begun to populate the Football League. Swansea City, a partially fan-owned club had even, briefly, made it to the Premier League. Upward progression felt inevitable.

As a boost to this sense of momentum, the movement also, finally possessed what it had long lacked, a genuinely 'bigish' club owned by the supporters. Portsmouth might not have carried the heft of a Manchester United or a Chelsea but with a stadium that held 20,000 and a pedigree that in recent memory boasted several seasons in the Premier League and one piece of silverware in the form of the FA Cup, they represented a quantum leap in terms of fan ownership when compared to others who had embraced the model. Here at last, so activists hoped, was a club that might have what it takes to take supporter ownership into the higher reaches of the pyramid.

Sadly, it didn't turn out like that. After a brief dalliance with fan control, the trust at Portsmouth sold out in 2017 to the Tornante Company, which was owned by Michael Eisner, the former CEO of Walt Disney. In the end, the limited finances available to the club, a frequent reality of supporter ownership, combined with a palpable desire to get back to the upper tiers of the pyramid, where fans thought Pompey should naturally reside, meant that a new owner promising the power to spend proved hard to resist.

Portsmouth's move away from fan ownership seemed to rob the model of some of its momentum. Although several trusts have embraced full supporter control in the years that followed the publication of *Punk Football*, and others gained a minority share, the movement remains broadly fixed within the parameters that framed it a decade ago. As was the case back then, supporter ownership, whether total or partial, has remained a largely non-league phenomenon, with a small foothold in the Football League.

And yet, recently, interest in fan ownership has received an unexpected boost. It arose as a consequence of the revulsion felt by fans towards the proposed creation of a European Super League (ESL) by the game's elite clubs in the spring of 2021.

When the ESL was put forward, it was met by fierce opposition, uniting considerable swathes of the football world against it; fans, football media and the game's governing bodies, such as UEFA, the Premier League and the FA.

There was a pervasive sense amongst the opposition that the game was being stolen in some way, thieved by those whose only interest was the bottom line. Ignoring the irony of bodies like Sky and the Premier League arguing that football was about more than money, the idea of a game being stolen carried plenty of weight. The ESL did represent a heist of sorts, a planned robbery by a small gang of clubs and the investment bank, JP Morgan that would, if taken to its logical conclusion, effectively see the separation of English football, decoupling its elite, money-making cadre from the remainder below.

But it would be one that was both entirely legal and one that the people who owned these clubs had every right to do. And perhaps it was that realisation that caused such disquiet amongst supporters, the fact that for all the press releases about understanding 'heritage', 'tradition' and 'what this club means to the fans', the people who own and run Liverpool, Manchester United and their ilk genuinely could not care less about 'heritage', 'tradition' and 'what this club means to the fans'. The modern football myth in the higher reaches of the game, of the benevolent owner, who despite his disconnect from the fanbase in terms of geography and provenance still loved both them and the club was shown for the sham it had always been.

Inevitably, not just amongst the rebellious clubs but elsewhere in football, the ESL threw attention on how we govern the game, specifically how our clubs are run. How much different would it be, many asked, if football was owned and run by those on the terraces? Surely something as patently monstrous as the ESL would never have been allowed to blossom by fan owners or even thought up in the first instance?

Of course, nothing is straightforward in football and for the advocates of fan ownership, it was a slight inconvenience that both Barcelona and Real Madrid, each key drivers in the creation of the ESL, are member-owned. But, within an English context, where our clubs have been run along private lines pretty much since the professional game's inception, it was perhaps inevitable that the question would be asked.

What's more, beyond acting as a bulwark against the proposed creation of the ESL, many advocates of greater fan ownership were putting forward the argument that the model could address other problems afflicting the sport, such as widening inequality, escalating ticket prices and financial gambling, the latter of which can frequently threaten the very survival of a club.

If fans had run clubs and the game, they pondered, could a very different version of English football now exist? Maybe it would be one where football was affordable to all, where the money the sport makes was more equitably distributed, where clubs understood that reckless debt accumulation was in nobody's best interest.

With so much furore created by the breakaway league, in response the Government was eventually pressurised into launching its long-promised Fan

Led Review into football. This review was tasked with looking at a variety of problems afflicting the game, such as football governance, ownership regulation and fan engagement. Led by the former sports minister, grassroots coach and Spurs fan, Tracey Crouch, the review reported in November 2021. Its conclusions and recommendations form part of this book, an analysis of where the supporter ownership movement currently stands in the wake of its publication.

But more than that, this short book also looks at why our current dominant model of ownership exists, why modern football has placed such pressure on it and why football clubs actually matter.

Punk Football was always something I wanted to revisit. The ESL, an idea that has not gone away, has simply made that revisit more pressing. The creation of the first supporters trust back in 1992 was a revolutionary moment in English football, a profound reshaping of what it means to be a supporter. Its impact continues to be felt in our game today, as fans continue to ask themselves the question: could I do a better job of running things myself?

WHY IS OUR GAME LIKE THIS?

It once really was the People's Game. That's the strange truth about football in this country. You hear that term bandied about a lot in the modern era, usually to sell our game back to us. The Sky Sports media machine is frequently the lead offender, using the term to force its product down our collective throats. It's meant to make us feel connected rather than seeing the reality, that too many fans are now reduced to being armchair supporters, priced out of a sport that, specifically at the top is controlled by billionaires and broadcasters, with the 'People' nowhere near the equation.

But back when the professional game was first establishing itself in the late 1800s, it was genuinely watched *and* owned by the fans. Like so many amidst the vast network of amateur clubs that populate the nether regions of the English pyramid today, clubs whose ownership is often rooted in the community and founded on principles of democracy, during the latter part of the 1800s, when the sport as we recognise it was taking shape, football clubs, irrespective of size or standing, were mostly member-owned, open to all and governed by elected committees. It was a footballing utopia where the fan truly was king.

Take, for example, midlands footballing pioneers, Aston Villa. During the club's founding years, they were run by a nine-man management committee, with each position elected by Villa's 380 members. Around the same time, a few hundred miles further south at Woolwich Arsenal, who had been established by employees of the Royal Arsenal in the mid-1880s, a management committee of workers, elected by a membership dominated by working men ran every aspect of the club.

In the very early days of football, when businessmen were involved with clubs at all, in the 'bankrolling' capacity as we understand it today, it was usually because there was a connection with a place of work. Like at Thames Ironworks in East London, where the owner Arnold F Hills helped establish a club that would go on to become West Ham United. Although the side was run by its members, Hill provided it with a stadium (one of the most impressive in England at the time) and established a sports committee that insured the players against loss of wages resulting from injury.

Alongside these more formal relationships, there were also instances of local businessmen with an interest in the game throwing a few quid at clubs. One of the most notable early examples of this was Lancashire industrialist Sidney Yates, who got involved with his local club, Blackburn Olympic during the early 1880s. His contribution became notable because the money helped Olympic become the first club from a working-class area to win the FA Cup. Yates' funding, which allowed for things like systematic training and a better diet, played an important part in the working man's challenge to the primacy of the wealthy, middle class amateurs whose clubs had dominated the cup since inception.

But, ironically, it was exactly this working-class challenge to the primacy of the 'old boy' amateur clubs of the South, not just in the FA Cup but across the game as a whole that would eventually erode the dominant culture of community ownership within English football at the highest levels.

And it was a challenge centred around the issue of professionalism.

Since foundation in 1863, the ranks of the FA had been staffed by exclusively middle class, well-healed men, the kind who boasted full-bodied moustaches and a singular approach to football. It was an approach rooted in the 'Corinthian' ideal of amateurism. This shunned professionalism and monetary reward, believing that football should be played for the love of the sport alone. It was an opinion made easier to hold when, unlike your working-class counterparts, you had the luxury of greater leisure time, a healthy bank balance to support your footballing endeavours and the kind of diet and living conditions that a factory worker could only dream of.

During the 1870s and early 1880s, as football ballooned in popularity, the drive towards paying players in England amongst clubs from working class communities to address the dominance of the 'old boy' amateurs became irresistible. These clubs, predominantly in the North and the Midlands, quickly realised that bunging players a few quid was the easiest way to assemble more competitive sides. Whether through the increasing amounts derived from gate receipts or via the involvement of a benefactor (like a figure such as Sidney Yates), using the club's money to recruit the brightest and the best enabled them to compete on a more equal footing.

The Lancashire giants of the time, Preston North End, Burnley and Bolton Wanderers were amongst the first to flout the FA's prohibition against professionalism and the most vocal in their support for it to be legalised. They were also three among nine northern clubs who threatened to break away from the FA and form a rival football authority should their demand not be met and professionalism made legal.

Initially, the FA tried to hold out, fining some clubs and threatening the more consistent offenders with expulsion. From their perspective, these northern upstarts needed putting in place, an attitude driven as much by a sense of snobbery as it was a genuine belief that these sides were in the wrong. But the FA was fighting against an incoming tide, one that brought with it the very real possibility that their relevance amidst vast swathes of the game could be washed away.

In the end, faced with this bleak reality, the FA capitulated and in 1885 the professional footballer arrived.

When it came to raising finance for these new professional players, the first area of recourse for any club was its fans. And these were increasingly numerous. From being a sport watched by a handful of people when it first emerged, by the early years of the new century, the popularity of the game had sky-rocketed. During the Football League's first season in 1888, 602,000 people watched the fixtures between the country's twelve leading clubs. Just a few decades later, that figure had reached nine million.

Aware that demand for the sport was growing exponentially and that the greater the number of supporters that could be accommodated, the greater the income a club could enjoy (and by extension, the better players it could afford), football clubs began to construct purpose-built stadiums.

The sums involved in building stands and stadiums were often beyond anything that a members club could achieve through gate receipts, cash donations or subscriptions alone, leading many clubs to seek additional levels of finance.

One of the simplest ways to do this was to convert from a members club into a joint-stock company. For clubs, there were numerous advantages to this move. Aside from the fact that they could now issue dividend-paying shares, joint-stock companies also enjoy limited liability; meaning that if a club became insolvent, shareholders were not liable for any debts (a protection in law that makes would-be investors more willing to part with their cash).

Small Heath (who would later morph into Birmingham City) became the first club to travel down this path in 1888. Over the following decades more and more clubs followed suit and by 1921, 84 out of the Football League's 86 clubs had converted.

Although, in theory, anyone could buy a stake, shareholding never took hold amongst the vast majority of supporters. Not only was it frequently beyond their financial means, but there was also a limited culture of shareholding amongst the working classes. By contrast, local businessmen and professionals from the middle classes could afford to buy shares in considerable volume. And this, in turn, allowed them to gain influence at clubs, seizing vital positions on the board.

It meant that within the space of a generation, the ownership structure within the professional game changed beyond recognition, shifting from one defined by community ownership, working-class representation and fan power to one in which ownership was concentrated into the hands of a wealthy elite, albeit a wealthy elite drawn from the local fanbase.

In many ways, this shift was an inevitable one. The early drive for professionalism created pressures to which the joint-stock system presented easy answers. And not just for the clubs. For the men who ran the country's principal football authorities, the FA and the Football League, it was a move that made sense. Neither body had an ideological problem with the effective privatisation of the pre-existing model. It evidently didn't take long, it seems, for the FA to get on-board with the idea that 'money' should dictate the way in which the game was organised.

Importantly, this indifference was echoed by the fans too. There were no protests against the change and the loss of community ownership went largely un-mourned. For much of the professional game's history, no sense existed amongst working-class supporters that they had any right to 'own' the club.

Of course, this isn't to say that supporters always agreed with the board. Undoubtedly, chairmen could be unpopular and clubs could make decisions that riled fans. But there was never any sense amongst supporters, even in their moments of collective anger, that the system of ownership that had emerged should be challenged. The reality was, as long as football remained cheap and accessible, and their clubs in no danger of going bust, the overwhelming majority of fans were happy to let the men of business (and it was almost exclusively men) run things as they saw fit.

It likely helped, at least until the arrival of the Premier League, that those sitting in the boardroom did not seem too distant to those standing on the terraces. There were no representatives from reputation washing Middle Eastern states, no owners of foreign investment companies, no Russian billionaires. The people who owned and ran football clubs were often local-boys-made-good and members from the local middle-classes, motivated to get involved through a love of the sport or a sense of civic pride. Richer than the average punter, unquestionably, but their geographic ties and a pervasive sense that involvement was about more than just the bottom line meant fans could feel an affinity with them in a way that would be impossible today in the higher reaches of the game.

In the modern debate surrounding club ownership in this country, it often gets forgotten that the arrival of these private owners and the end of supporter control possessed not just its own sense of undeniable logic but also widespread acceptance amongst fans. We might lament the fact that clubs over here are not owned in the same way as those in places such as Germany, Spain and Sweden – where fan ownership is more common – but football developed differently in these countries. It was a difference that allowed the creation of a more interventionist fan culture to take hold. And much of this was because, in these countries, unlike England, the drive to professionalise occurred later.

'In Germany, for example, this didn't happen until the 1960s with the arrival of the Bundesliga' says Prof Kay Schiller, German sports historian at Durham University. 'Unlike in England' he continues 'where the sport was quickly embraced by the working-classes, in Germany at both club level and within the principal football authority, the Deutscher Fußball Bund (DFB), the middle-classes remained more dominant.'

For this class, like their English counterparts, professionalism was seen as an affront to the values of amateurism.

'But where the English old boys quickly lost

control of the game, in Germany the middle-classes managed to maintain a position of strength for a lot longer, giving the dominance of amateurism greater longevity' says Schiller.

Without the pressure to professionalise, the existing model of ownership, one that shared much in common with England's members clubs, was given the space to thrive and normalise. In Germany, this type of organisation is known as an eingetragener Verein (e.V) and tends to be the model adopted across many different sports. At its heart, it is a way of running football that embraces the concepts of democratic ownership and community benefit.

'Owned by the fans and run by officials elected by and accountable to those fans, this model became the norm within Germany. Because of this, supporters developed a very distinctive relationship with their clubs as the sport grew. No fan ever sees themselves as a mere customer. But in German football, this was even more the case as the fans were genuine stakeholders in the club. This meant that the concept of involvement being limited to simply paying to watch your team and little else became alien' says Uli Hesse, author of *Tor!: The Story of German Football.*

Even after full professionalism was introduced with the arrival of the Bundesliga in 1962, the supporter ownership model remained. 'It had become an indelible part of German football culture' Hesse continues. 'It was too established, too much part of fan life for the game to be run any other way. Although ownership has been diluted in recent years, albeit protected by the "50+1" rule to never fall below 51 percent, the Verein model is still dominant, along with the sense of supporters being something more than customers. In this country, the fan is king.'

Similar stories are told in other places where professionalism arrived later than it did in England. But our story was different. Here private owners got their hands on the game much earlier and once established, there was no way the men who had invested in English football were going to hand over control to the great unwashed (even if those same fans had wanted it). It's also a story in which, in the professional tiers, and even into layers of the semi-pro game, our democratic origins have become more and more distant as the years have passed. And not just in chronological terms. There is an undeniable sense today, most keenly felt in the Premier League, that the distance between the fans and those who own our clubs has never been greater.

This was best illustrated by the recent machinations of the so-called 'Big Six', who, in the Spring of 2021 attempted to join the rest of the continent's elite clubs in a breakaway European

Super League. The English clubs joining in with this plan bought into a scheme that sought to redefine supporters in the process, separating them into two distinct groups: 'Legacy Fans' and 'Future Fans'. The former, generally local to the club, older in age, more likely opposed to the scheme, were dismissed in favour of the latter, those usually younger, less geographically connected to their clubs and more open to the glitz and glamour that the new competition promised. This was the most naked example of football moving away from its origins, wilfully abandoning those communities that had built those clubs in favour of emerging markets elsewhere.

Although widespread fan outrage was credited in the thwarting of this attempted coup, which for some suggested that the influence of supporters had not waned as much as many in the game had feared, in truth the collapse of the plan had more to do with the broad alliance created in response than it did solely with notions of fan activism. It was an alliance that brought the fans together with disparate groups, including UEFA, Sky and the Premier League. Rarely natural bedfellows, there was a feeling amongst some involved with supporter activism that when another fully-formed scheme emerges again, and there seems to be too much money involved for this not to happen, should it be able to pick apart that alliance, by perhaps bringing opposition elements, like Sky, on board, no amount of fan anger will prevent some form of Super League from becoming a reality.

'The truth is that football is changing' says Martin Cloake, football writer and co-chair of the Spurs Supporters Trust. 'When we talk about "fans" today, we have to embrace a much wider definition. Clubs like Liverpool and Man Utd have millions of supporters worldwide, many of whom will pay subscriptions to watch their team. Equally, these clubs could probably sell thousands of seats every weekend with tourists coming to watch a "football experience". Set against that, you start to realise that the "old" fan, or I suppose "Legacy" fan if you want to use the elite's language, is not as important as they used to be in the higher reaches. We still matter, obviously, but that degree is probably diminishing. And I suppose that is the logic behind the super league.'

Of course, it's not just the proposed ESL that has illustrated the growing disconnect between fan and club/owner. Take ticket prices. For most of the game's history, football, at any level, was cheap and it was accessible. That was part of the reason why so many supporters were happy with the existing ownership structure. But in recent decades, throughout the game, but specifically at the top, that is palpably no longer the case. Since the Premier League arrived in 1992, for example, the cost of going to a top-flight match has risen at some clubs by as much as 1,000 per cent. To put that into context, if the price of day-to-day items had increased in line with Premier League ticket price inflation, a loaf of bread would cost £18 today.

This sense of a sport becoming increasingly out of reach financially is expressed elsewhere too. It's there in ever-escalating kit costs (Chelsea, £120 – Tottenham, £120 – Liverpool £119) and in clubs charging north of a tenner for a pie-and-pint. Taking the kids to the match, once something open to families of almost every income, has become a luxury event in the Premier League, something that when food and drink are taken into account can easily cost more than £100 at some clubs.

'There is little doubt that many fans in the modern game feel like they're little more than numbers on a balance sheet, there to be endlessly milked by a club. That sense of connection that once existed between the club and the supporters is possibly not as strong as it once was, particularly at the top. That's not to say that fans don't love their club, they obviously do. But perhaps, and this is probably more keenly felt in the Premier League and the Championship, there is undoubtedly a feeling of disconnect that now exists between some supporters and their clubs, which is probably an inevitable consequence of feeling exploited' argues Martin Cloake.

For many, the manifold problems that now exist within football are rooted in the pernicious influence that 'money' has had on it. Of course, 'money' has always influenced the professional game. There have long been wealthy men willing to take a punt on a football club. The people behind early professional pioneers, like Preston North End, Burnley and Bolton Wanderers understood that. Deep pockets inevitably enable you to get the jump on rivals. In professional football, despite what misty-eyed romantics might say, there has never been some socialist utopia of financial equality.

And yet, undeniably, in the pre-1992 world, the stakes were not nearly as high as they are today. Football, in the higher reaches, has moved from the world of the moderately wealthy to the world of the indecently wealthy, from the local-boy-made good to the investment arms of Middle Eastern states. The days of Sidney Yates throwing Blackburn Olympic a few quid to prepare for the FA Cup final seem a very long way away by today's standards.

Inevitably, as more money has flowed into the game, much of it concentrated at the top, the gap between the 'Haves' and 'Have Not's' has widened. This is an inevitable consequence of any poorly regulated market – and English football over recent decades has been free-market economics at its most naked. Inevitably, inequality has boomed, creating in the process a tiny elite at the top who hoard as much of the money as they can and who dominate the titles, cups and European places available.

In the 'Football League' era, a relative minnow like Wimbledon could power up the divisions and one day beat the leading side of the day in a FA Cup final. In those same days, a club like Watford could go from the depths of the Fourth Division to second-placed in the First. And in that halcyon age, clubs like Burnley, Derby County and Nottingham Forest could still claim the top prize. Although anything is still possible in football, the chances of a League Two minnow rocketing up the divisions today and challenging for the title are exceptionally unlikely, unless that same minnow was fuelled by the bottomless pockets of their billionaire owner.

The key moment in this shift was the arrival of the Premier League in 1992. As the new division signed a £304m five-year TV deal with Sky, few could have known back then that the seeds had been sown for the creation of an entirely new form of football. Fast forward thirty years and, at the time of writing, it is thought that the Premier League's current TV deal, covering 2022-25 will hit the £9bn mark (when foreign broadcast rights are included). Those billions will only add to a trend that has been in effect for three decades, the enrichment of an elite and the continued distortion of English football.

'There is little doubt that the money that has been pumped into English football in recent decades has changed it. Although apparent at every level of the professional game, it's been more keenly felt at the top. And it's a trend that has been intensified by other changes to the ways that club earn money and attract investment, such as the transformation in the income that can be earned from participation in European competition and the arrival of a new generation of staggeringly wealthy owners', says Kieran Maguire of the Price of Football podcast.

The Champions League, a competition that the English elite has had a lock on since it was created can now bestow millions on teams, even if they only make the group stage. For teams that go all the way and win the thing, which the likes of Manchester United, Chelsea and Liverpool have managed, they can nowadays expect to bring home around £75m in prize money, plus many millions more in broadcast revenue.

This seasonal largesse has been complemented by a change in the profile of those who now own our football clubs at the top (verging in many instances to those possessing what is best described as 'f**k you' money). Through the likes of Sheikh Mansour and until recently Roman Abramovich, the money pumped into English football has been considerable. It's estimated that

Chelsea previously owed Abramovich around £1bn. Manchester City accounts show Sheikh Mansour has poured roughly £1.3bn into his Etihad dreams. These are sums that would have been inconceivable a generation ago.

The ramifications of this considerable influx of money have been felt everywhere. 'Take transfers and wages' says Kieran Maguire. 'Premier League clubs are now, collectively, regularly spending hundreds upon hundreds of millions during each window, with records seemingly broken year by year. And, when it comes to wages, some Premier League annual average salaries are now exceeding £3m a year. Although definitely skewed towards big clubs, the median level is still £2.5m.'

But this phenomenon is not confined to the top-flight. Perniciously, the impact of money trickles downwards. In 2017/18, for example, the Championship saw a record wages/revenue ratio of 106 per cent. Figures for the two divisions below, while not as dramatic, nevertheless point to a system in which inflation and unsustainable wage spending has become the norm.

'One of the strangest aspects of modern football is the fact that despite all this money flowing into the game, at every level of the sport clubs are still regularly spending more than they have. Inflation has just pushed costs up further and further, leading most owners to spend more than they have, just to compete. It turns out that whatever deals are brokered and however much is earned, it's never enough', says Andy Holt, owner of League One's Accrington Stanley.

That's why ticket prices continue to rise and rise. And not just at the top. It now costs around £25 to sit and watch a League Two club, £15 to stand in a dilapidated terrace to watch a side at Step One. It's also why the lucrative corporate market has swelled, why clubs have so many commercial partners and why there is a morally neutral approach to sponsorship that has seen so many clubs take a tainted shilling from the gambling industry.

A pervasive desire now runs through football that seeks to milk fans as much as possible and to sweat the club for all it is worth.

And yet, despite unprecedented levels of income, for many clubs, debt has become a way of life. In the Championship, collectively it currently stands at around £1bn. Of the existing debt, just over three quarters have come in the form of 'soft loans' from owners. It illustrates how many clubs continue to be heavily funded by their owners, usually underwriting transfer and wage spending that the business could never conceivably afford.

This problem continues as you travel down the pyramid. According to the most recent accounts from several clubs in Leagues One and Two, Coventry currently owe £42m to their owners, Colchester £22m, Fleetwood £13m, Bristol Rovers £13m, Southend £13m, MK Dons £10m and Chesterfield £10m. And these represent just a handful of the many indebted clubs that populate the bottom two tiers of the Football League who, in the absence of some rare stroke of good fortune, like a particularly beneficial bit of transfer business, have no real capacity to ever pay this back from their existing revenue streams,

'The problem with football today is that the riches on offer as you edge up the divisions, specifically the Premier League, are so tempting that owners will do anything to get there. They'll take massive financial risks. But then, if they do reach this promised land, it's not like the spending and risk-taking stops. They then have to continue in this manner just to stay there. And because there is so much money sloshing around nowadays, as you head upward the sums required to take these risks and maintain this spending have just got larger and larger. Too many of these owners don't see themselves as "custodians" of a vital community asset. Instead, through vanity or incompetence, they treat clubs like playthings, and chase "success" at all cost, sometimes with disastrous consequences', says Andy Holt.

English football is now littered with stories of clubs

that have gone into debt or staked their futures on the promises made by a new owner all in the hope of making it to the next level, whether that be promotion to the Championship, entry into the Premier League or a push for a European place.

The issue for many clubs is that such is the price demanded to become competitive, it all too frequently fails. For every Manchester City, there are so many more Portsmouths, clubs whose business model never had what it took to match their lofty aims. The tale is a familiar one, generous transfer spending, a ballooning wage bill, all of it covered by soft loans or unsustainable bank debts. And then, when the footballing success, and its accompanying promise of riches, does not materialise, the whole thing collapses.

Damningly, despite the riches the sport has been able to generate in recent decades, more than 45 clubs have fallen into Administration in the last 20 years. Many more have come perilously close. In fact, according to figures recently released by Fair Game (a collective of clubs committed to improving the governance of the national game) over half of the top 92 clubs in England were technically insolvent in 2020.

Most of the stories that surround these sorry tales of financial woe are depressing, often caused by a combination of overreach and incompetence. But perhaps none are as depressing as that which occurred in the summer of 2019 when the accounts of one club got so bad that they ended up being expelled from the Football League.

'No one wanted to be in this position but following repeated missed deadlines, the suspension of five league fixtures, in addition to not receiving the evidence we required in regard to financial commitments and a possible takeover not materialising; the EFL Board has been forced to take the most difficult of decisions', so said Debbie Jevans, the EFL's executive chair outlining the reasons why on 27 August 2019, Bury FC were removed from the Football League, bringing to an end 125 years of continuous membership.

The origins of Bury's sorry tale lay in the tenure of the club's penultimate owner, Stewart Day, who took control of the club in 2013. Day subsidised the loss-making Lancashire side with loans from his property company, Mederco. But Day was no Sheikh Mansour, able to endlessly bankroll the club through bottomless pits of money. When his main business got into trouble, the cash dried up and Bury, unable to pay the players or anyone else, came close to bankruptcy.

With Bury on life support, they were sold in December 2018 for £1 to Steve Dale, a man who at no point illustrated to the EFL that he had the financial resources to rescue the club. Despite this, his takeover went ahead.

Dale later claimed that he did not appreciate just how bad the problems were at Gigg Lane, an admission that did little to help the club. Although Bury survived a winding-up order just a few months after he had taken it over, the writing appeared to be on the wall. As the season wound to a close, the list of creditors and the amount owed swelled, with the latter standing at around £8m according to *The Guardian*. The players and coaching staff had also not been paid for months.

During the summer of 2019, against a background of a worsening financial picture, the club entered a company voluntary arrangement, meaning they would face a twelve-point deduction for enduring an 'insolvency event'. Although bad enough, worse was to come. Bury never got to start their campaign. The club's ongoing financial problems led to a series of suspended games, compelling the EFL board to meet a few weeks into the season to discuss the crisis.

The club was given a 5pm deadline to complete a sale. C&N Sporting Risk, a sports analytics firm waited in the wings, poised to take over. But its offer never came. C&N withdrew around 90 minutes before the deadline, baulking at the scale of the financial problems facing the club. The failure to complete the sale would ultimately mean that Bury became the first team to be expelled from the Football League since Maidstone's liquidation in 1992.

On expulsion, the club's players had their contracts invalidated, making them free agents. It left Bury a club without players, without its coaching staff and without a league to compete in. All of this while also trying to grapple with a crippling level of debt, with limited means to generate the necessary income to pay it back.

For many fans, what happened at Bury merely represents one more entry to add to the long list of crimes that modern football has visited on supporters. Whether it's escalating ticket prices, financial catastrophe or elite clubs trying to wrestle the game away from the rest, there is a pervasive sense amongst many that the sport would be in much better health if the clock could be turned back 150 years and our clubs returned to the hands of the fans. After all, who better to understand why a football club matters so much and why its protection and survival is so important than the people who turn up week-in-week-out to support it?

WHY DO FOOTBALL CLUBS MATTER?

In many ways, football was lucky. It came to life at just the right time.

During the closing decades of the nineteenth century, as the game we recognise today was emerging, changes were taking place in society that would greatly benefit the nascent sport.

After decades of exploitation under the brutal assault of industrial capitalism, working men and women in Britain were beginning to fight back. 'New Unionism', which differed from the 'craft unionism' of the past by embracing unskilled and semi-skilled workers, such as dockers, factory workers and general labourers was becoming a force in the country.

Its wider reach and a willingness to flex the movement's muscles in the form of industrial action gave some working men and women greater power within economic society, leading to tangible benefits, most notably better wages in certain industries and more leisure time at the weekend. This latter development, the creation of the

Saturday half-day, played a pivotal role in football's expansion, at both professional and amateur levels. Having Saturday afternoon off not only enabled working men to play this new game, but it also meant that millions of them were ready for a form of entertainment that could occupy their recently acquired leisure time. And that's exactly what football would provide.

But the sports ability to become the nation's favourite pastime, morphing from a game that was watched by a handful of adherents when it first emerged to one beloved by millions was about more than simply arriving during an era when working people had more time on their hands and a few quid in their back pockets. Football also offered spiritual nourishment.

As the working classes flocked to watch football, the grind of the working week weighing heavy on their shoulders, they found a collective experience qualitatively different from the isolated life of the home or factory.

Urban workers in the late-nineteenth century were still, to a large extent, only a generation or so removed from their recent agrarian past, rooted in farm labouring and village life. Cut off from the traditional securities this world provided - the extended family, the familiar faces of the 'parish' - they suffered alienation in the impersonality of town life and industrial competition. Along with pubs and music halls, Saturday afternoon football games made possible a new sense of belonging.

The arrival of the Football League in 1888 assisted in this process. The regimented and frequent nature of the League's matches helped provide a greater focus for collective urban leisure in industrial towns and cities. And as the clubs involved began to flesh out a distinctive sense of place within the wider framework of national competition, they tapped into notions of localism and civic pride too.

Teams were named after a town (Liverpool) or district (Everton). Some clubs claimed to represent the 'City', whilst others brought together followers under the banner of 'United'. In smaller towns, working men could direct their interests towards one team. But in several larger cities, like Liverpool, Manchester and Sheffield, two-club rivalries became the norm. The League's 'derby matches' between neighbouring sides offered the opportunity to determine who ruled the locality both in a sporting and in a wider symbolic sense. Bragging rights have always mattered.

As too did the 'culture' of the terraces, such as the emergence of *blason populaire*, a folk tradition within the working classes whose origins stretch back centuries. Expressed through songs, chants and insults, it was a tradition that embraced the denigration of outsiders and revelled in stereotypes. It's easy to see how football fed into this, a sport that lent itself not just to feelings of 'community' but also notions of in-group and out-group. As the industrial revolution slowly eroded the traditions of rural life for many, football chants stepped in to replace the older forms of *blason populaire*. For the working classes, its appeal was obvious, tapping into concepts of 'self' that had long permeated their culture.

This was joined in later decades by the 'collective chorus' of those assembled, something that accentuated the feeling of belonging that football offered to the working classes, that 'imagined community' attendees yearned for. Although the 1960s is often heralded as the age where pop music bled into the terraces, creating the singing culture that we recognise today, in truth its roots reach much further back. Those early crowds would sing popular songs from the time, specifically the 'hits' from the music halls. Some have even stood the test of time, like 'Blaydon Races' at Newcastle United and 'I'm Forever Blowing Bubbles' at West Ham. These songs allowed working men to hark back to a pre-industrial age, a time when larking and singing formed part of daily life. The practice had retreated under the impersonal assault of the factory, enjoyed only patchily through the pub and the music hall. Football gave another opportunity, a chance to reconnect.

The Victorian and Edwardian working man, and his successors in the decades that followed, long appreciated the sense of community that football offered, underwritten by elements like the cathartic hostility of the crowd and the feeling of togetherness provided by communal singing. It all fused to foster a sense of loyalty and dedication that has forever surrounded the sport. When Bill Shankly spoke of a game that was more important than life or death, he was tapping into a feeling that was widely understood, one that was formed during the early decades of the professional game. Football mattered, instilling a level of dedication that made its adherents suffer for their love.

This was why, in the era of relatively meagre incomes before the Second World War, fans would walk vast distances in their dedication. At Everton, there are tales of supporters making the trek from Bootle to Goodison Park and back on foot, a round trip of ten miles, so devoted were they to the club they followed. Other fans did something similar, walking equally challenging distances, such was the near-palpable desire to be at their 'churches' come 3pm on a Saturday. And when they got there, wearily entering the ground, they put up with football's inhospitable environment. The stadiums might have moved on from the built-up earth banks of the game's origins but the leap was hardly a stellar one. The windswept concrete terraces, the crush of the crowd, the absence of comfort. Although admission was cheap, it reflected the experience.

But you had to be there. And not just because in a pre-TV age this was the only way to consume the game. You had to be there because there was nothing else like it. Shankly might've had his tongue ever-so-slightly planted in cheek when he uttered that immortal phrase, but there was a kernel of truth there. Football spectatorship was an unmatched experience that became hugely important, an experience that could reframe your mood for the week to come, that could move you in ways ordinary life could only hope to achieve.

Although the sport has unquestionably evolved in the century-plus that followed those origins, much of the template of fandom has arguably not. The 'go to the game' mentality that still characterises concepts of 'fandom' today, where those who physically attend see themselves as superior fans compared to the armchair army at home, has its roots in the ideas of what constituted a true 'fan' formed during the era of mass working-class embracement of football. They were those who did what it took to be there because being there, physically, mattered.

Equally, fandom has remained more than just a commercial activity. 'It is an ongoing sensual process' writes Dr Mark Doidge in *Ultras: The*

Passion and Performance of Contemporary Football Fandom. 'There is an intertwining of the self with the club. It becomes a Durkheimian totem that symbolises the self within a community. As one of the many football clichés goes, no one wants to have their ashes scattered in a supermarket, yet millions of fans have done something similar at their team's football ground. Emotion is one of the enticing and intoxicating aspects of watching and playing football.'

And it's not just positive emotions that shape this relationship. Recent research by the University of Oxford has revealed that significant losses shared with fellow supporters represent an essential element of 'fandom' too. Like famous victories, they bind fans together more tightly to one another and their club. Painful losses can be so intensely felt that they are perceived as 'self-shaping' experiences, meaning they become embedded in the psyche of a football fan so that their own identity fuses with that of their club. Over time, such shared experiences only further increase our loyalty to our teams.

Increasingly, this sense of loyalty has also become one of the few surviving remnants of the old, pre-individualist world. During much of the previous century, loyalty to a football club represented just one element of a person's web of connections to other communities. A working man or woman might have the local pub, the local church, the trade union. Much to the fury of Thatcherites, there was such a thing as 'society', specifically amongst the working-classes. Working people saw the benefits of collectivism, recognising its worth in shielding them from the impersonal assault of the market.

That is less the case in Austerity England. Although communities still exist, the certainties of the past are no more. We live in a more fractured society, where the individual is prized above all else. For many, that collectivist world seems alien by today's standards, a modern world where you might never talk to your neighbour, where trade unions might no longer exist in your workplace, where going to church is only something pushy middle-class parents do to get their kids into their school of choice.

Set against this, the 'imagined community' of the football club becomes even more vital. It is the place people go to feel connected, to experience something that modern England so infrequently provides. It's the sense of being part of something, of being in a space where the whole is so much greater than the individual. Just because the factories have mostly gone and our lives have become more comfortable, doesn't mean that the 'imagined community' football provides isn't still important. So many of the reasons why people were drawn to football many years ago are still applicable today. In fact, in the face of an increasingly fractured society, some of those reasons have only become more compelling.

And that's why, 150 years on, football still matters massively to those who follow it, creating a sport that is arguably, in sheer numeric terms, more followed today than at any point in its history. Modern football consumes followers in a way that few other interests can, occupying the thoughts, dreams and fears of millions all day, every day. It remains, as Arrigo Sacchi so memorably said, 'the most important of the least important things'.

Key moments in a club's history, like Liverpool's comeback in Istanbul in 2005, Manchester United's last-gasp turnaround against Bayern Munich in 1999, Aguero's injury-time goal to seize the title for Manchester City in 2012 form an essential part of the collective memory, the foundations upon which the 'imagined community' of the 'fan' are built.

This concept of the 'fan', an individual who despite underlining their relationship with a club via a monetary transaction is, nevertheless, so much more than a simple 'customer', has long been understood across the sport. Fandom, if it has an equal, is more akin to religion, a near-dogmatic, unshakable, sometimes inexplicable sense of faith.

But even beyond the emotional pull and sense

of belonging that clubs provide, there are other reasons why they matter so much to people in this country.

To begin with, they are economic engines. In 1991/92, the last season of the old Football League, the 22 clubs in the top division had collective revenues of £170m a year. By the 2018/19 season, the collective turnover of the 20 Premier League clubs had increased to £5.15bn. In the second, third and fourth tiers of English football, collective revenues have increased from £93 million in 1991/92, to just under £1bn in 2019/20.

This economic activity makes clubs key drivers of growth in local areas. A recent report on the economic and social impact of the Premier League undertaken by Ernst & Young picked out West Ham United as a useful example of this.

According to the report, through the club's role as a major employer, its spending with local businesses, and the thousands of visitors it attracts during an average season, West Ham significantly impacts the local economy of East London and Essex. In 2018/19, the club contributed a total of £300m in Gross Value Added (GVA) to the regional economy. To break this down:

- The club supported 3,300 local and regional jobs, nearly 50 per cent of which

were residents of boroughs local to the club.
- Almost half of total supply chain spending is sourced from local suppliers, equating to £15m.
- Over 50,000 away Premier League supporters visit the London Stadium, bringing additional spending into the local economy.

But beyond this economic importance, there is also the community role to consider too. In his article, *'The death of the 72? Why football outside the Premier League is on its knees'*, Miguel Delaney, Chief Football Writer at *The Independent*, wrote:

'Football clubs are not just, well, football clubs. They are local social institutions. In many lower-league towns, in fact, football is now the sole true community hub. Even local authorities and police forces lean on these clubs, as they are increasingly rare places where people gather.'

This role is particularly evident in distinct community outreach units that almost every professional club, and several semi-professional clubs, now possess. Known as Club Community Organisations (CCOs), these off-shoots work within the community to address a range of problems, such as educational deprivation, social isolation and low levels of physical activity. And the impact they can have is impressive. Back in 2020, an EFL analysis found that in one year, £62m is spent directly on community and social projects collectively by its member clubs, reaching just under 900,000 people.

The location of football clubs and their widespread (and demographically diverse) popularity also gives them a reach that the average charitable programme would struggle to achieve. As the EFL point out:

'...The reach of EFL Clubs and their CCOs is huge. In turn, the programmes and engagement opportunities offered by CCOs can be genuinely life-changing. People who live in the catchment areas are more likely to have lower physical activity rates and are more likely to be overweight or obese than elsewhere. Earnings are frequently below average. This means the sport/physical activity programmes delivered as a mainstay of Club CCOs' offerings can be hugely beneficial... Overall, the scale of the impact in sheer numbers alone, along with an ability to reach into the country's more deprived communities and engage difficult-to-reach groups at, what appear to be, cost-effective and value-for-money rates, points towards CCOs providing a highly effective route to community engagement.'

But a club's impact on the social welfare of the local

community is not restricted to the 'charitable' work they undertake. It is also the case that football clubs can have wider social benefits.

'In many towns across Britain the football club is by far the dominant institution, often comparable to the position once held by the church', explains Peter Starkings, co-author of the report, *These Clubs Are Ours*, which recently examined the case for greater supporter ownership in football for the community charity, Power to Change.

'Clubs' he continues 'provide venues for weddings and birthdays, host food banks and, during the Covid pandemic, vaccination centres. Club legends encourage local children to work hard in school and lead public service messaging. These intangible benefits are, in fact, the stuff of life. Clubs are places where friendships are made and life events are marked. They retain a special power like nothing else.'

They are also institutions that can play a vital role in how a community views itself. As Kieran Maguire puts it in *These Clubs Are Ours*:

'Football clubs are unique in that they give an individual town or city an identity and a sense of belonging, which doesn't exist in anything else. It doesn't matter if you're Leave or Remain, it doesn't matter if you're Labour or Tory, you have that common bond. It gives you an opportunity to engage with people. If you take away what football represents in terms of that identity, you're reducing further the opportunity for people to come into contact with each other and you're going to further accelerate the gaps and the divisions that we already have.'

At times, football can even grow to inhabit the hopes and dreams of an entire place. Towns and cities can be energised when a club does well, a galvanising effect that lifts all. These Are Our Clubs highlighted this with the case of Wolverhampton, a city that for many decades was 'a byword for de-industrialisation and poor socio-economic outcomes'. Set against this, the report argued, the recent success of Wolves, which has been powered by the investment of the club's new owners, Fosun International, has seen it become an obvious focal point for civic pride. As Wolves progressed up the pyramid, eventually establishing themselves as a Premier League fixture, the colours of the team have 'swamped the city'.

'The value of football clubs to both fans and local communities is immense' says Peter Starkings. 'When a club does well, it can give the entire town or city a lift, restoring pride and boosting a sense of community. And equally, when a club goes under, which happened at Bury, and has happened in parts of the non-league game, it's felt at a fundamental level, not just by the fans but also by others in the local area. I think that's why you've seen such an expansion in supporter activism in recent decades. People know that football clubs are not invulnerable and the game as we know it today can wreak devastation if a club gets in the hands of the wrong kind of owners.'

As Starkings mentions, the once universal passivity of supporters, that sense that a club's running was best left to wealthy individuals who have everyone's best interest at heart, is no longer quite so pervasive. In both a response to the material threat that many football clubs now face and also a reflection of the growing alienation that fans feel in today's game (priced out, disenfranchised, unable to identify with a new generation of owners), during the past thirty years, a more activist culture has blossomed within our national game.

THE RISE OF SUPPORTER POWER

The first stirrings of this 'activist' trend emerged during the death throes of the old pre-1992 football world. It was seen in the explosion of the fanzine movement in the late-1980s, in the fan-led campaigns against far-right infiltration at clubs like Leeds United and West Ham, and in the founding of the Football Supporters Association (FSA) in 1985, an organisation created by fans to campaign on issues that mattered to them.

'People often think of the late 1980s and early 1990s as a dark time for football. And in many ways, it was. This was the post-Heysel-era, the time of the European ban when attendances were at an all-time low and the reputation of fans, tarred by hooliganism, was rock bottom. And yet, for the first time in the sport's history, you begin to see supporters becoming more politicised. That sense amongst fans that the club and the people who ran the sport knew best was starting to unravel' says Rogan Taylor, co-founder of the FSA.

Why this occurred has as much to do with wider

societal trends as it did a reaction to what was happening in football itself. Deference, the feeling that your social 'betters' had a right to govern, was on the wane in the country at large. As too was the post-war consensus, the agreement between the Government and the forces of capital and labour that had delivered full employment, rising living standards and a social safety net during the 1950s, 60s and 70s. As Thatcherism began tearing apart the certainties of the post-war world, the 1980s became a time of political upheaval, a time characterised by a strong reaction amongst individuals and communities to a rapidly changing social and economic landscape.

'Inevitably, a bit of that fed into the football world. But equally football fans were developing the sense that they could do things themselves. I think a little bit of that was rooted in the 'do it yourself' aesthetic that had arisen from Punk and was evident in other subsequent music scenes. The fanzine movement was certainly inspired by that. As too were the anti-racism campaigns. There was a feeling that if the club programme was crap, and they almost universally were, why not make your own? Or if the club or the FA won't do anything about the National Front, then why couldn't other fans act' says Paul Thomas, one of the founders of Leeds Fans United Against Racism and Fascism.

As the 1980s bled into the 1990s, this sense

of proto-activism grew further. Campaigns at club level and supporter politicisation began to proliferate more widely across the game. It was a trend that gradually matured into the Independent Supporters Association (ISA) movement, which emerged during the mid-1990s. Faced with a game that was changing rapidly, but not always, from the perspective of the fans, in a welcome fashion, ad-hoc campaigns began to search for a more stable and consistent medium for organisation and representation.

'And they found this in the ISAs' says Andy Walsh, a key figure behind the creation of the Independent Manchester United Supporters Association (IMUSA). 'The problem in the 1990s was that it often wasn't just one problem affecting supporters, you were facing issues on multiple fronts. The arrival of the Premier League changed football beyond recognition, creating a sport beset with systemic problems, many of which impacted upon fans. Rising ticket prices, clubs going bust, the arrival of owners disconnected to the fanbase. The problems that we see across the game today were just starting to be felt back then. Fans, for the first time in the sport's history, were beginning to feel disenfranchised. This, and the widespread nature of the problems faced, meant that some kind of medium for supporter representation was probably inevitable.'

The ISA's promised to give supporters a voice, a chance to fight back against the forces that many felt were taking the game away from the very people, the working-class fans, who had underwritten football for over a century.

'It was a medium that proved to be invaluable for us in the late 1990s as we organised to fight an adversary who threatened the very soul of the club' says Walsh.

The threat to Manchester United came from Rupert Murdoch and his attempt, via his broadcaster, BSkyB, to purchase the club in 1998.

'We knew in our hearts that he would be bad for the club. He would destroy it. There was this sense that there was a material threat to the future of the club we loved. So, we had to organise and fight back' recalls Walsh.

IMUSA, with broad support amongst the fans, launched a campaign that targeted figures from the worlds of the media, politics and high finance. When combined with hostility to the bid from other organisations involved in football broadcasting, such as the BBC, the Independent Television Commission and the Premier League, they collectively helped convince the Government to refer the takeover to the Monopolies and Mergers Commission for consideration. They, in turn, rejected the bid.

'To say we were jubilant would probably be an understatement' says Walsh. 'This wasn't just an example of supporter power in action; this was an example of supporter power succeeding against one of the most powerful figures not just in English football but in English society too. At the start, plenty of people wrote us off, thinking that we didn't stand a chance. And you can understand why. This was Murdoch after all, the man who tended to get whatever he wanted. But we persevered, we organised and ultimately we triumphed.'

The Murdoch affair, along with other fan-led campaigns at the time, revealed just how far supporter activism had travelled in a very short period. Supporters were now willing and capable of challenging clubs and in doing so, altering the way that these clubs were run. As the 1990s came to a close, the momentum was now with greater activism. Although there were still plenty of fans who cared little about the politics of football, a growing (and increasingly vocal) section of supporters were beginning to think that fans had a right to have a say in how their clubs were run. And their ability to organise and do this would receive a significant shot-in-the-arm as the decade came to a close with the arrival of Supporters Direct.

A few years earlier, in 1997, Tony Blair's first Labour Government had roared into power, fuelled by a thumping mandate and sparkling with an energetic commitment to reform. Although football had undergone something of a renaissance during the 1990s, shedding its reputation for crowd violence and undergoing a process of 'gentrification' in its higher reaches, it was still a sport beset by problems. Racism, escalating ticket prices, friction between supporters and clubs, were just three of the many issues affecting the game. An industry so in need of reform was never going to escape the attentions of New Labour and not long after taking power Blair's Government launched the Football Task Force (FTF). Drawing on representatives from all sectors of the game, the FTF was charged with the remit of finding solutions to the problems that still afflicted football.

Although it never turned out to be as radical as many supporters had hoped, the FTF did have a lasting and enduring impact on the game. Many of its recommendations on issues such as racism, disabled access to stadiums and the improvement of links between football clubs and their surrounding communities, were acted upon by the Government. But arguably its greatest impact was the decision to recommend the creation of a body that could take fan activism to the next level through the creation of football trusts, supporter-run organisations whose aim it would be to hold clubs to account and promote the concept of fans ultimately owning and running the teams they followed.

Oddly, considering how much Government activity was devoted to football in the 1990s, the idea for these trusts didn't originate from some Westminster think-tank or the ideas-board of a sharp-suited management consultant. Instead, the foundations of the trust movement were laid by a group of Northampton Town supporters. Back in 1992, at the same time that the newly arrived Premier League was ushering in a revolution in the English game, a few fans of The Cobblers were bringing in a revolution of their own.

The man behind this simple yet revolutionary concept was Brian Lomax. Brian, who is no longer with us, spoke to me a few years ago, while I was working on my first book, *Punk Football*:

'When my daughter was old enough', he said, 'I began thinking about taking her to watch one of the local football teams play. We had a couple of choices nearby, but the one that had the 'hometown' feel that I really wanted, the feeling which was similar to that which existed at Altrincham, who I'd followed as a boy, was Northampton Town. At first, it was just home games but, as time went on, we started going away too because it was so enjoyable.'

But by the early 1990s, a cloud had descended upon the County Ground. Under the disastrous ownership of Michael McRitchie, Northampton were making a loss every month and had managed to rack up £1.6m worth of debt. With the club in Administration, the prospect of it being wound up loomed menacingly.

'It was clear as the financial crisis deepened and time passed that nobody was coming to save us, no white knight charging to our rescue. In response to this, a few of us arranged a meeting of the supporters to see what could be done' explained Lomax.

The meeting was called in the town on a January evening in 1992, attended by 600 fans (tightly packed within a building designed to hold just 250). A representative from the club informed the assembled crowd about the extent of the problem, including the fact the club wasn't even able to pay the players' wages at that moment in time.

Lomax had been asked to chair the meeting because of his political past, which had seen him stand for election four times as the local parliamentary candidate for the Liberal Party:

'The idea of forming a fan-owned trust that would invest in the club was floated during the meeting. A few of us had talked about this beforehand after I'd brought the idea up. The option and need were there for some fundraising body to be created. But I and some others felt that this should be one that got something in return for its investment and one that could look after any money the fans raised.'

According to Lomax, support for the trust idea was given a boost when, during the meeting, those assembled were provided with a stark reminder of how supporters had been treated in the past when they'd last raised money for the club.

'One of the chaps who attended showed us a blazer badge given to his dad in the fifties when Northampton fans had bought the first floodlights at the club, which had cost them a lot of money. What the supporters got in return for their considerable investment was six blazer badges and the opportunity for the chair of the supporters club to have a drink with the club's big-wigs once a year.'

By the time the meeting was closed, the Northampton Town Supporters Trust (NTST) had been established. Initially, it had two basic aims (1) to raise money to save the club and (2) to seek effective involvement and representation for supporters in the running of the club to ensure that such a catastrophic situation could never occur again.

The trust was organised as an Industrial and Provident Society (IPS). Legally, these organisations fell into two broad categories, a cooperative (run for the benefit of its members) or a community benefit society (run for the benefit of the wider community). Both categories enjoyed limited liability, which meant the personal liability of the society's members was limited to the amount of their unpaid share capital.

(Since 2014, via the introduction of the Co-operative and Community Benefit Societies Act, all such societies have to register either as a Co-operative Society or a Community Benefit Society. Societies previously registered as an IPS can currently call themselves Registered Society or Industrial and Provident Society. However, if they want to become a CBS or a Co-op Society, they have to re-register)

This share capital in these societies was not made up of equity shares like those in a joint-stock company, which appreciate or fall in value with the success of the enterprise that issues them. Rather they were par value shares, which could only be redeemed (if at all) at face value. The share typically acted as a 'membership ticket', and voting was on a 'one member one vote' basis.

According to Lomax, the inspiration for the development of NTST had come from the Mayday Trust, the housing organisation that he ran in Rugby.

'It struck me that an organisation such as that

seemed the perfect vehicle to provide supporters with the opportunity to come together to buy a part of their club and act as a medium through which fans could democratically influence club policy. I didn't see any reason why what worked elsewhere in society couldn't be translated to football. I also felt, and this was based upon my experience of running the Trust, that the more you enfranchised people, the more responsibility you gave them, the more effort they put in.'

Once formed, the NTST set about raising cash for its aims. Fundraising efforts began spontaneously in pubs, clubs and workplaces, and dozens of individual donations ranging from £1 to £1,000 were received. A bucket collection at the first home match after the Trust was formed yielded £3,500, over £1 per head of the gate. Through these efforts, the Trust was eventually able to raise £30,000, enough for it to buy a stake in the club and have two elected directors on the board.

This convinced the Administrator that Northampton could return to solvency. The existence of the Trust, and specifically its fundraising capacity was given as the main reason why the club could be viewed as a rescue prospect. When the Administrator convened a meeting to organise the future management of Northampton, a new board emerged with four former directors and two representatives of the NTST (each elected by the Trust).

What happened at Northampton was hugely innovative. But because of the club's lowly position in the hierarchy of English football, it only received a fraction of the media attention that other examples of fan activism in the 1990s commanded. And nor did supporters take much notice of it either. Despite several clubs undergoing bouts of financial crisis during the decade, with several coming close to going out of business, the trust model remained something that existed on the margins of the game.

And yet, although few within the ranks of those responsible for running the game had taken an interest in Punk Football's emergence, the story of Northampton Town did prick the curiosity of some of those charged with modernising football, most notably the current Mayor of Greater Manchester, Andy Burnham.

Burnham, active in the 1990s as a researcher for both the Labour Party and the Transport and General Workers' Union, had, in 1997 taken up the post as an administrator with the FTF. He spoke to me about this for *Punk Football* back in 2013:

'I was very aware of what had happened at Northampton and was impressed by the good work they were doing. Northampton was turning into a really progressive club, working hard to tackle many of the problems that were affecting other, traditionally owned clubs. The more I delved into this issue the more evident it became that a big reason for this progressive approach was the role being played by the NTST, which was acting as a vital connecting link between the club and the supporters.'

Burnham and the FTF started to look into the mechanics of the supporter trust model, talking over its foundation and role at Northampton with Brian Lomax. They concluded that the model could represent a panacea to many of the problems that the game was facing.

Andy Burnham: 'Having supporters on the board could change a football club. Not only could fans tell the board what supporters wanted, but they also had the power to do something about it. Our view was that if this model could be promoted elsewhere in the game then perhaps football could start to be reformed from the bottom-up, with supporter power acting as the agent of change.'

At the time, the FTF didn't have the power to do anything about it aside from making a recommendation to the Department of Culture, Media and Sport (DCMS). Fortunately, the DCMS was about to be joined by somebody who was very receptive to the FTF's recommendations, as Burnham explained:

'In 1998 I was appointed as a special advisor to Chris Smith, Minister at the DCMS. So, in effect, I became part of the audience to whom the FTF's recommendations were made. Needless to say, I worked hard to have them accepted.'

With the help of Smith, in 2000 the DCMS launched Supporters Direct. Its mission was to promote sustainable sports clubs based upon community ownership and supporter involvement, to publicise the benefits of the model and also provide support and advice to individual clubs and groups of supporters wishing to establish trusts of their own.

According to Dave Boyle, who worked for Supporters Direct between 2000-2011, acting as chief executive for a time (2008-2011), those involved with the new organisation were heartened and surprised by the response of the fans following the launch.

'Our initial business plan forecasted us helping establish around 50 supporters trusts in the UK. But it soon became clear that demand massively exceeded expectations. I think the reason for this is that we came at the right time for supporters and with a message that was appealing. Fans were becoming more politically active, a reaction to how the game was changing so much. The advent of Sky and the Premier League was remodelling football, tearing apart the traditional relationship between fan and club in the process. Ticket prices were rising, clubs were spiralling into debt, the whole notion of 'going to the match' was altering. Football supporters as a group were unsettled by this.'

At the same time, fans had witnessed what supporter-led action could do; learned by the examples of what happened at Northampton Town and Manchester United during the 1990s.

'So, when Supporters Direct came along, promoting the idea that if united, fans could not only have a better chance of influencing their club but potentially buy a stake in it, or even own it completely one day, it evidently struck a chord' says Boyle.

But although the fans were very responsive, initially this wasn't the case with the chairmen and owners.

'The attitude was one of 'what do they know about running a football club, they're just supporters' said Andy Burnham, who not only helped found Supporters Direct but also acted as the organisation's chair during the middle part of the 2000s.

'Although fairly parochial on this issue, the response of owners and chairmen was hardly a surprise' he continued 'after all, despite the growing politicisation of supporters, few had ever claimed that they had a right to run the club and until Supporters Direct arrived on the scene the concept of fan-ownership was confined to the margins of the game.'

But the dismissive nature of some owners gradually began to change as the number of trusts actively involved in running clubs started to grow. And during the early 2000s opportunities for a trust to grab a stake were plentiful. Administrations were happening at an unprecedented rate and although many clubs were rescued by 'white-knights', not all were so lucky. The trust model promoted by Supporters Direct offered these unfortunate clubs a lifeline, one that was eagerly grasped.

Andy Burnham: 'Quite early on several clubs, like Exeter, Swansea and York City got into financial trouble and found that the only way they could survive was with the help of the supporters. Through their work in saving these clubs and then being involved in how they were run, several owners began to realise that perhaps supporters did know something about the business after all. It wasn't an overnight conversion and it certainly wasn't comprehensive but there was a definite softening of opposition and a gradual acceptance that there could be something to this new idea.'

Since it was established in 2000, Supporters Direct, which merged with the Football Supporters' Federation in 2018 to form the Football Supporters' Association, has assisted in the creation and subsequent support of over 100 supporters trusts in English football. During the past two decades, the face of the English game has, in no small part, been shaped by this activist movement. There are clubs with long storied histories that only exist today because of a trust. There are clubs that have been brought into existence through the collective power of the fans. And there are clubs that have been dead and buried only to rise, phoenix-like from the ashes with the energy of the supporters fuelling their resurrection.

And these, are just a few of them...

THE CLUBS

LEWES FC

Since foundation, it's fair to say that Lewes FC have rarely set the non-league world alight. Aside from a smattering of lower league trinkets, their unquestioned highlight was elevation to the National League for a single season back in 2008/9. Although, even the joy of that success proved short-lived. Lewes ended their sole campaign at Step One rock bottom of the league and on the verge of financial ruin.

'It was a familiar story' says current Lewes FC chairman, Stuart Fuller. 'Overspending to chase success, a lack of the required financial infrastructure to cope with life at the higher level, progress on the pitch probably happening too quickly. The whole mess conspired to leave the club in a dire state and facing the strong possibility of going under.'

But the crisis ultimately ended up presenting Lewes with the chance to take a different, and increasingly revolutionary path, as current Lewes director, Charlie Dobres explains:

'For a time back then, it looked possible that the

club would be wound up. And that would have been it, over a hundred years of history gone in the blink of an eye. Luckily for us, the fans would not let that happen. A group of supporters known as Rooks125 [a fusion of the club's nickname and its age at the time] took control of the club and then worked to transfer Lewes out of private hands and into community ownership.'

'To achieve this' he continues 'we appealed to the fan base. In year one, we limited the ownership offer to Life Shareholders who could give £1,000 or more. Through this, we raised well over £100,000. We did it this way as our immediate issue was addressing the debts the club faced. We needed a lot of money very quickly and the "Life Shareholders" plan delivered on that score. But, after that, we opened ownership out to anyone who wanted it, with prospective owners initially buying a share in the trust for £30 per year.'

At the moment, Lewes have around 2000 owners. Standard membership comes in at £50 a year (although there are more expensive packages for the more committed). Irrespective of how much you pay, that share gives the holder a single vote in club matters and the right to stand for the board.

Despite the healthy number of investors, not bad for a club that is only averaging around 750 through the gate, according to Charlie Dobres, being competitive with this model remains a daily challenge.

'Although the club does benefit from some Directors each year making good losses, so that Lewes never has any ongoing debt, we always budget to break even without any Director contribution. And we have also enacted a strategy to move towards full self-sufficiency on reliable annual revenues (with membership representing the core element of this). But we are often competing against clubs who aren't run like that. Clubs who might have a wealthy benefactor underwriting ongoing losses, sometimes significant in scale. They can operate in a way that we can't, specifically with playing budgets. And that can make life hard.'

Turning Lewes into a Step One club under this model, which is a stated aim of the board, will be a challenge. The absence of an external cash injection means that the club has to do things differently, to innovate. Fortunately, this is an area where the club has excelled in recent years, specifically in creating a unique 'brand' at their home, the Dripping Pan, one that Lewes are trying to leverage to broaden both those choosing to support the club and those willing to become shareholders.

According to Charlie Dobres, being fan-owned forms part of this. 'When you're competing for the attention of fans, and here I'm not just talking local non-league clubs but also clubs in the Football League and the Premier League, being community-owned can set you apart to a degree. There are lots of fans out there who are feeling disenfranchised from football, especially in the Premier League. Our progressive style of ownership speaks to them, bringing Lewes a level of attention that would be perhaps denied to a more conventionally owned club at this level.'

Although this helps the club position itself favourably in a crowded marketplace, on its own it is not enough. Partly because as a 'USP', it's not as unique as it once was. There are currently several clubs in England where supporters have some form of control (several of which are completely owned by the fans). Indeed, just a few miles from Lewes, in places like Eastbourne, Tonbridge and Peacehaven there are non-league clubs run this way.

'And so, you have to do more' explains Dobres. 'You have to build your brand, build on what separates you from other clubs and what makes you special.'

Several adjectives have become associated with the club since the fans took over, such as quirky, progressive, inventive. What they all add up to is the sense that Lewes do things differently. The 'sell' for fans is that by following or investing in the club you are getting the chance to be part of something beyond the norm.

This unique 'brand' comes at you, the prospective fan/owner from a few different angles. Lewes' match-day posters are the stuff of non-league legend, some of the best of which adapt film publicity posters, tailoring them to their opponents, such as Halloween becoming Harloween (Harlow Town), Eraserhead becoming Leatherhead, and Stargate for Margate.

Then there's the 'corporate hospitality'. 'This started as an April Fool's idea but in the end, turned out to be one of the best things we've done' says Dobres. 'We have a few beach huts at the home end that now function as our corporate boxes. For £100, six punters get food, a minibar, free wifi and a match programme, along with the best view in the house'.

The 'corporate hospitality' at the Dripping Pan, forms one part of a match-day experience that has seen the stadium name-checked alongside the likes of Signal Iduna Park, Camp Nou and the San Siro when it comes to rating the best grounds to visit in Europe. Indeed, it even, recently, claimed the top spot in Mike Bayly's critically acclaimed book, *British Football's Greatest Grounds.*

And it's easy to see why the ground wowed Bayly and numerous others. Aside from its setting, gloriously nestled amidst the South Downs, the Dripping Pan offers everything you would want from a non-league game, the friendliness, the sense of community, but with a twist. Whether it's the beach huts, the broad and eclectic playlist broadcast over the tannoy (The Fall, Aphex Twin, CAN) or the tea bar that sells the best pie and mash you've ever eaten, you're getting to experience something worth the trip, something that you might not get somewhere else.

But as important as the above is, perhaps the move that has truly set Lewes apart from the crowd was the decision back in the summer of 2017 to remove the funding disparity that existed between its men's and women's sides.

The plan forms part of Equality FC, the club's wider campaign that aims to raise awareness about gender inequality in the sport and encourage more support for women's football across the UK.

'Although the picture has improved in recent years, there is still a sense in football that the women's game is somehow lesser. We wanted to change that', says Fuller. 'At this club, we believe that there should be a level playing field for women in football. And that's why we decided to commit to paying our women's and men's teams equally, to provide budget parity. By doing this we hope to spark a change across the UK that will help put an end to the excuses for why such a deep pay disparity has persisted in football.'

When Lewes announced this new approach, the

club made headlines, with features appearing in the likes of The Guardian, The Times and on the BBC. And the story's reach did not stop with the UK. What Lewes have done has brought an international focus, a rare degree of media attention for a club of this size.

'Despite deciding to do this because we think it is the right thing to do, the move has really pushed our brand to a wider audience. We have seen an upturn in membership, more people coming to our men's and women's games, and a broader range of partners want to be associated with the club. People want to be part of what we are doing here, and Equality FC is a big part of that' says Dobres.

Budget parity and Equality FC have cemented Lewes' reputation as the most revolutionary club in English football. For Stuart Fuller, being fan-owned has played an integral part in this:

'I'm not sure we would be the club we are today if we weren't community-owned. It's opened us up to new ideas, new ways of "doing" football and given us more creative freedom. Although there are struggles and downsides to fan ownership, I think the club has benefitted enormously from the change. I would not want my football club to be run in any other way.'

AFC WIMBLEDON

Back in 2000, The Milton Keynes Stadium Consortium (MKSC), a group led by the developer, Pete Winkelman, put together a proposal for a large commercial and retail development in the town.

A key element in this was a 30,000-capacity football stadium. But that came with one glaring problem, the fact that Milton Keynes lacked a local club that could fill anything more than a 100th of the proposed ground. In response, Winkelman got creative.

He began looking for struggling clubs that could be lured away from their spiritual homes, tempted by the chance to play in a brand-new stadium and to enjoy the bountiful pleasures of Milton's Keynes innovative grid road system.

He eventually found his potential saviour in South London. At the time Wimbledon were in trouble. Massively in debt, no ground to call their own, and with the club's Norwegian owners looking to off-load, the offer from Winkelman to buy the Wombles and relocate them to Milton Keynes came at an opportune moment.

'We had a lot of problems at the club but almost all of them were rooted in our lack of a ground', says Ivor Heller, current commercial director at AFC Wimbledon. 'Our old stadium, Plough Lane, had been sold off to Safeway. The previous owner, Sam Hamman had flogged it when it became clear that the club didn't have the money to upgrade it to meet the recommendations of the Taylor Report.'

After the sale, Wimbledon had entered into a ground-share with Crystal Palace at Selhurst Park. But the problem with any ground-share is that they very rarely benefit both sides equally. And Wimbledon's deal was no exception. The club was unable to enjoy the same financial benefits that Plough Lane had provided, such as those relating to commercial partnerships, sponsorship and matchday revenue. Faced with declining revenues and rapidly increasing costs (attributable to the wage spiral that was beginning in the top-flight following the creation of the Premier League), the club began to lose money heavily.

'And this continued even after Hamman sold up to new owners, Kjell Inge Røkke and Bjørn Rune Gjelsten. The new regime lacked the capital necessary to underwrite the club and losses mounted. In simple terms, we just couldn't make enough to cope with wage inflation because the club barely brought in any revenue. When the Milton Keynes offer came in, promising to buy them out, clear the debts and provide the club with a new home, the owners thought it was like a gift from God. Unsurprisingly, they accepted' says Heller.

And with that, for the first time in the English professional game, franchise football became a possibility. The fans inevitably protested, taking their case to the Football League, believing that sanity would prevail. As if to illustrate from the very beginning that this would not be the case, the League brought in the FA.

The pair put together a panel to consider the matter. It sat for four days, taking contributions from both sides, eventually being won over by Winkelman's 'infectious enthusiasm'. When the final judgment came, it left the supporters crushed. The move would be allowed, meaning Wimbledon would be severing their 113-year association with South London.

The betrayal, which was officially sanctioned by the FA on 28 May 2002, left Wimbledon's fans with a wretched choice, stay true to their first love and commute a 100-mile-plus round trip to watch them play or switch allegiances altogether to another London side, the latter representing the ultimate sin for any football supporter.

'The choices offered were unpalatable, to say the least' Heller explains. 'No fan should be presented with a choice like that. Fortunately, we came up with a third option ourselves, which was to start a new, local club that was owned by the supporters. In reality, it was the only option that made sense. The version of "Wimbledon" that had moved to Milton Keynes was no longer our club. And there was no way we could have started watching another London side.'

Founded in the immediate aftermath of the move, the new club was to be owned and run by the fans under the aegis of the Dons Trust, a supporter led IPS. The Trust, utilising its membership subscriptions, provided the club with the immediate means to raise finance without recourse to outside parties, such as banks or local businessmen. Through this, they were able to cobble together enough money to pay for a squad of players and cover the costs of moving into a groundshare at the Kingsmeadow Stadium, home of non-league Kingstonian. All they needed now was a name:

Ivor Heller: 'We had a meeting with the London FA where it was going to be decided what the club was to be called and establish its founding date. We half-jokingly put forward Real Wimbledon as a name, which was met with a definitive 'no'. In the end, AFC Wimbledon was accepted, even though the AFC part doesn't really mean anything. When it came to our founding date, I cheekily suggested 1889, the same date that Wimbledon FC had been established. To my surprise and immense satisfaction, this was accepted, something I am eternally proud of.'

AFC Wimbledon opened their campaign in the Premier League of the Combined Counties Division, Step Five of the National League system, against Sandhurst Town on a blisteringly hot summers' day in August 2002. Keeping in mind that back then, the average gate for games in this league was around 100 people, the travelling army of 2500 AFC Wimbledon fans presented something of a logistical challenge. They surmounted this by the ingenious idea of cobbling together a makeshift stand built from hay-bales, which provided the opposition fans with sufficient if fairly uncomfortable seating to watch their new club earn three points following a 2-1 victory. It was a win that would set the tone for what was to follow.

'It took us a few years but eventually, we got back to the football league' says Ivor Heller. 'We went from open trials on Wimbledon Common, to county football, to the Conference and then to the Football League, eventually ending up in the same division as the other club, MK Dons. And we were powered on that journey by our amazing fans and the Dons Trust. Without the support and funding of both, we would have just been a footnote, a nice idea that didn't work out, probably languishing in the lower tiers of the National League system. But as it is, we have hopefully shown what is possible with this model.'

Through it all, AFC Wimbledon have been very careful, never overspending and once in the Football League becoming that rarest of beasts, a club without debt.

'We've progressed steadily and conservatively' says Heller, 'resistant to both debt and outside investment. Other clubs have done what we have done in a much quicker period of time but done it by spending heavily and having a benefactor on hand to cover losses. Our progression might have been slower but it was sustainable. And it's got us to a point where we have been able to compete while staying true to those principles of sustainability' says Heller.

The club has also recently come full circle by moving back to the Borough of Merton, once the home to their beloved Plough Lane. Funded by the club and a community bond scheme, the latter raising £7.5m, AFC Wimbledon now boast their own 9,300 capacity stadium in the heart of their ancestral borough.

'For us, the move completes the journey' says Heller. 'The loss of our ground is the reason why the hated move came about in the first place. There is a sense of justice about building our new stadium back in Merton and having this fan-owned club complete the project. It's taken us pretty much a generation to get back here but the way that we have done it proves that supporter ownership can do great things. And it also shows those in football who abandoned us all those years ago, like the FA and the EFL, that you should never write fans off because, collectively, we can do amazing things.'

CLAPTON CFC

Clapton Community Football Club was only formed in 2018, but its origins can be traced back to 2012 when a group of fans, priced out and disillusioned with Premier League football, decided to venture into the non-league world and lend their support to Clapton FC.

With tongue only partially planted in cheek, they became known as the Clapton Ultras, bringing not just greater numbers to the club's terraces, swelling attendances from the low tens to as high as 400 on match days, but also an energy that had long been absent at Clapton's Old Spotted Dog ground.

'We were bringing the noise and energy that you see in the Ultra culture in Europe to Clapton. Singing, chanting, the flags. For a lot of us, it was about reawakening that terrace culture that used to form part of English football but which has died out in the higher reaches of the game. We were also political in our outlook, something that is common amongst continental Ultra groups. We were, and remain, avowedly anti-fascist and we did, and do, a lot of work for the community, helping out local food banks and publicising the cases of marginalised people' says Kevin Blowe, one-time Ultra and current treasurer at Clapton CFC.

For a time, the symbiosis between the club and the Ultras worked. The former benefited from the rise in attendances, the latter from somewhere to call home. But the partnership was not to last.

'Several flashpoints developed' says Blowe. 'Membership of the club was closed by the chief executive Vince McBean, effectively shutting out the Ultras and the wider community. There were also price hikes, the introduction of heavy-handed security and McBean's desire to sell off some of the club's assets at a time when he faced formal investigations by both the Charity Commission and the FA'.

An Ultra-led supporter boycott of home games began during the 2017-18 season in protest at McBean's governing of the club.

'Lots of us involved in the boycott felt that the club had become isolated from the community. To us, the obvious answer was to start a new incarnation of the club, one that went back to the membership model that had served Clapton so well for over one hundred years. The idea, in essence, was to have continuity. The new supporter-owned club would be, from our perspective, a continuation of the old community-minded one, with democratic ownership at its heart.'

In 2018, the Life Members at Clapton FC voted with the wider fanbase to establish a functioning members' club that would be open to all, boasting transparency and inclusivity as its key values. The new club, christened Clapton Community Football Club, which began life in the Middlesex Counties Football League, the eleventh tier of English football, marked the formal separation of those committed to democratic accountability and those, like McBean who were left behind.

Unlike other clubs, even those that are fan-owned, Clapton CFC do not have a standard and traditional top-down board structure. Instead, they have established several semi-autonomous committees drawing on a wide range of experience and expertise across the supporter base – and transparency runs through all of their work.

'We've done away with the position of chair,' Blowe says. 'There's no need for it. We encourage our members to help us run the club. We're committed to being open – our argument is the more eyes you have on an issue, the more questions being asked, the more likely you are to spot problems that might develop down the line.'

Since its inception, steady progress on the pitch has been more than matched by progress off it. The left-wing, community-minded ethos of the

Ultras has become an indelible part of how Clapton CFC functions. Whether it's offering 'pay what you can afford' girls football to low-income migrant families, campaigning to raise money for Medical Aid for Palestinians or allowing community charities to take over the club's social media platforms, this is a club that has stayed true to the political perspective of the Ultras.

Allied to this, the club has also recently taken great steps to lay the foundations for a more secure future by acquiring the freehold of the Old Spotted Dog. Before this, they had been groundsharing with Walthamstow at Wadham Lodge, affectionately nicknamed by fans as the 'Stray Dog'. The chance to obtain the freehold of their original ground arose in 2019 and following a vote by the members at the club's General Meeting, it was unanimously agreed to make an offer, backed by a loan from Cooperative & Community Finance.

Kevin Blowe: 'Bringing Clapton's spiritual home back into community use was absolutely central to the motivation for setting up Clapton CFC. Finally having a ground of our own, owned by members, will offer long term stability for the club and also provide the chance to build lasting links with the local community.'

The ground was, and remains to some extent, in serious need of renovation and repair. But, as is frequently the case with supporter-owned clubs,

Clapton CFC have been able to call upon a volunteer army to lick it back into something approaching 'shape.' With the ground back in action, Clapton, at last, have an important resource to generate revenue, something that is vital for a club that does not have a 'sugar daddy' to turn to.

Not that, in the absence of their ground, the club wasn't already illustrating to the football world its nifty commercial footwork. This was revealed back in 2019 when Clapton were able to sell a phenomenal 15,000 replica away shirts. The design of the shirt was inspired by the colours of the International Brigade, those who fought against fascism in Spain during the civil war in the 1930s. The shirt features the slogan 'No Pasáran' (they shall not pass) which was used by Republican troops at the time.

'The club had originally expected to shift just 250 shirts that year! So, shifting thousands has been a massive boost' says Blowe. 'Things like that matter to clubs like ours, those that are owned by the community. We don't have a deep-pocketed benefactor to turn to. We live within our means and that means we have to get creative on the business side. But although it can sometimes make life harder for you, it's the best way to run a club. To be owned by the community, by the people who actually come and watch the club, that's how football should be.'

FC UNITED OF MANCHESTER

Before he arrived at Manchester United, few people had ever heard of Malcolm Glazer, unless of course, you were one of those rare few in this country with a passing interest in American Football. Glazer, who made his fortune from an eclectic array of businesses, including real estate, nursing homes and oil, became the owner of the Tampa Bay Buccaneers in 1995. Under his stewardship these perennial under-achievers have enjoyed periods of unparalleled success, the high points being their clinching of the Super Bowl in 2002 and 2020.

First and foremost a businessman (Glazer has presided over a tripling of the Buccaneers' franchise value since taking control), according to advisers he became attracted to the idea of taking over Manchester United because of his belief that the owners were under-exploiting the brand.

Glazer and his family, through their company Red Football, purchased their first tranche of United shares, a three per cent stake in March 2003. This was then built up in the two years that followed until, in June 2005, they were able to pass the 90 per cent threshold enabling them to compulsory purchase the remaining shares.

The sale would introduce many English fans to a new financial term: the leveraged buy-out. Essentially, the Glazers were able to buy the club with £525m of debt that would then be serviced by the club, so United would effectively pay for them to become owners.

For a small group of United supporters, the financial chicanery of the takeover would prove to be the final straw in their deteriorating relationship with the club.

'There was an element within the fanbase, many of who had been involved in the IMUSA, that were increasingly disillusioned with life at Old Trafford' says Andy Walsh.

For years this 'element' had been campaigning against several of the changes that had been taking place at the club.

'Rising ticket prices, heavy-handed stewarding, the commercial exploitation of fans, it felt like the "United" of our youth was slowly being replaced by this corporate monster' says Walsh

And then came Glazer.

'For a group of us', he continues 'enough was enough. The debt-funded buyout was a step too far.

So, we began to look at ways we could register our disgust with the club. One way was our custom. People like Glazer always assume that fans will take any treatment meted out to them. They look on us like a herd of sheep that will meekly turn up season-in-season-out, regardless of the despicable way that the club treats us. It was one of the hardest decisions of my life but I felt that the only way that we could make our feelings known was to challenge this assumption and to say we won't come through your turnstiles and you're no longer getting our money'.

But amongst many of those who decided to withhold their custom from the club, there was also the sense that the Glazer affair represented an opportunity. The idea of starting a new club had first been mooted by the IMUSA during the proposed BSkyB bid. It was regarded at the time as a 'nuclear option', the fans last resort should Murdoch become their new owner. Over the years that followed, the rumbling discontent with the way that United was run ensured that the idea never really went away. By the time Glazer took over, a significant cadre of United supporters, the majority of whom were actively involved in the influential fanzines, Red Issue and United We Stand, were ready to go 'nuclear'.

'In 2005 a group of us began talking about the feasibility of starting a new club. At first, it was probably just talk but we kept coming back to it again and again and realised that there were enough of us seriously committed to the idea to give it a go. And in June of 2005, that's exactly what we did. We knew that we needed to be robustly organised, so in an eight-week period, we established a steering committee of 15 people, started to actively recruit members, developed a business plan, looked into finding somewhere to play, drew up a constitution and made an application to the FA and the Football League to participate as a new club' says Walsh.

If one word could be said to define the steering committee's business plan in those early days it would be unrealistic, but unrealistic only in the sense that they underestimated just how popular an endeavour FC United would be. The initial business proposal was based upon the assumption membership would be around one thousand; an estimate that turned out to be exceptionally cautious.

'Within a few months FC United had raised £180,000 from around 3000 members and although the club did get some large investments of around £5000, much of what was raised came in small amounts' says Walsh.

Like other supporter-owned clubs, F.C. United constituted as an IPS. Currently, membership is obtained by paying a £15 annual fee, with each of the club's members (roughly 2500) receiving one share and one vote, regardless of the amount paid.

Since its foundation in 2005, FC United have thrived. On the pitch, they have moved from the nether regions of non-league football to its higher reaches, even spending a few seasons in the National League North. One of the best-supported clubs outside the Football League, FC United of Manchester have been able to create a fanbase almost from scratch, building successfully on those who departed Old Trafford with them.

But it's probably off the pitch where the club truly excels. As FC United of Manchester website proudly boasts:

'We have a principled commitment to be of benefit to our local community and to work with everyone in the community through an inclusive ethos that resonates with our membership. We are passionate and understanding of the wider role that football clubs can play in assisting communities local to them. Our community programme is varied and not exclusive to football or sport – 'we do things differently' and our community programme is evidence of this.'

This community angle is there in the digital inclusion classes run for the elderly, in the school sports sessions it provides for young people and in the work the club does with refugees in the community.

'From the beginning, FC United was about community. In fact, the club is first and foremost a community organisation, something that comes before football' says Walsh. 'The idea was to create a different kind of football club, one that was not just democratically owned but also one that served the community it lived in.'

A key element in being able to do this was the building of the club's new ground, Broadhurst Park in 2015. The club raised millions through community shares to help fund its creation. The 4,400-capacity stadium shows what can be achieved when football fans with a vision work together and make things happen. FC United's members were involved at every stage during the design and construction process. As a community facility, Broadhurst Park is now used every day by local people and hosts a range of sporting, social and recreational activities.

The story of FC United of Manchester is a remarkable one. All too often, fan disgust towards an owner dissipates. You saw that perfectly during the summer of 2021 when open hostility towards owners like the Glazers, Stan Kronke and FSG during the ESL debacle quickly melted away as fans refocused their energies on what was taking place on the pitch. But back in 2005, the outrage at United was channelled into something tangible, creating a lasting alternative to the original club, a place where those disillusioned with life at Old Trafford could go. And for the rest of us, a wonderful example that football could be done differently.

BURY AFC

Remember Bury? The club that will remain forever a cautionary tale for overreach and appalling football governance. Well, rather than let this dreadful tale of financial woe be the final point of the club's footballing journey, the fans rallied to open a new chapter. Expulsion from the Football League was not to be the end. Through supporter power, new life was breathed into the town's football story.

'When the club folded, there were still lots of people in Bury who wanted to watch a local football team. People might look at where Bury is and think, "Why don't they just go and watch City or United". But this is a town with a long history of having a local football team rooted in the community. Why wouldn't they want that to continue? And so, perhaps inevitably, the idea of a phoenix club emerged and a few of us got together to see if we could make it happen' says Phil Young, chair of the Shakers Community Society, the supporters trust that owns Bury AFC.

Like almost all supporter owned clubs, timing was

essential.

'We knew we had to move quickly' Young explains. 'You want to bring people with you and in that moment, in the wake of the expulsion, there was a lot of goodwill that could be capitalised upon and a lot of interest in what we were doing. Would that be the case a year down the line? We weren't so sure. You'd always probably have a core who would remain open to the idea, but to make a club viable you really need as many people as possible. So, for us, moving quickly was important.'

And that's just what they did. In just a few months, with the help of the FSA, the new club had appointed a manager, the former Sunderland and Leicester winger Andy Welsh, agreed a groundshare with the Northern Premier League club Radcliffe and secured a place in the pyramid, the 10th level, in the North West Counties League First Division North.

'People might think that the hardest part of setting up a new club is the financial side', explains Young. 'But although that is a challenge, it was the bureaucracy that was the main hurdle for us. Even something like setting up a bank account for a community benefit society was not straightforward, largely because football clubs owned and run in this way are not that common.'

When establishing the club, the trust undertook a

sample survey of the fanbase to assess what they wanted from this venture going forward.

'It probably comes as no surprise' says Young 'that "financial security" topped the poll. I think a lot of supporter owned clubs are like this. So many are formed in response to a financial crisis that fans understandably want to ensure that this never happens again. With Bury, that feeling is even greater. We know what it's like to effectively have your club taken away from you because of how badly it was run.'

Unlike most fan owned clubs who tend to pitch their membership costs at a relatively low level, the Shakers Benefit Society have opted for a different approach.

'This ties in with our past' explains Young. 'We used to be known as the "bucket shakers", a reference to how often the fans had to shake buckets outside Gigg Lane to raise money to fund the club. We don't want the fan owned version of Bury to be like that. And so, we thought, better to price membership properly, which is £60, than to pitch lower and have to go back to the fanbase again and again. We want this club to be run properly, which I think, again, goes back to that desire for "financial security" that the fans wanted'.

Although the timing of the club's launch was slightly unfortunate, coinciding with the pandemic and its associated cancellation of grassroots football, Bury AFC adapted well to the challenging circumstances.

'On the one hand, you're trying to build a fanbase and connect with the community and not having matches taking place affected that. However, we have a great media team who spent the lockdown really pushing our brand and our story, resulting in decent shirt sales and increased membership. So, strangely, when you combine that with the fact that we had no player costs, that period without football actually ended with us being really profitable', says Young.

Since football's return, things have gone well for the club on the pitch. Back in April 2022, in front of a crowd of 1,885 – echoing the year Bury FC were founded – the first trophy of a new era was secured when they were crowned champions of the North West Counties League, Division One North.

'What we've achieved this year has been absolutely massive', manager Andy Welsh said to *The Guardian*. 'My players are not on thousands of pounds a week. I've demanded a lot out of them, but they have really bought into it.'

Many of these players have dropped down a few levels to play for Bury, attracted by the big crowds and the sense of a club that is run differently.

'I think our story is one that people are buying

into' says Phil Young. 'It is an impressive one. We have around 300 volunteers who have put so much into this club to get it to where it is. When you consider what could have happened in Bury, that football in the town could have simply died, you really appreciate how vital all that work has been. The success on the pitch merely adds to that. And from here we hope to grow as a club and hopefully continue our progress up the pyramid.'

But where this future football will be played is still uncertain. Gigg Lane, home of Bury FC was recently bought by a consortium led by fans group Est 1885, along with the club's trading name, history and memorabilia.

Following the buyout, talk in the local media and amongst fans was of a possible fan-owned club playing its football back at the club's spiritual home. However, according to Phil Young, that is not guaranteed.

'We don't want to move back there just for the sake of it. Any move we make in the future has to be sustainable. There are problems with Gigg Lane that potentially make that an issue, so we will have to wait and see. While it remains a preference, if a move is not in the best interests of this club, specifically if it threatens that notion of "financial security", then it won't happen. For us, this was never about getting back to the EFL or getting back into the ground. This was about creating a community football club in the town that people could feel part off and which did things differently to the club we lost. And that's exactly what we have at the moment.'

Despite being relatively new members of the punk football community, Bury AFC's story is an inspirational one. Few fans in English football have been dealt a hand as bad as that given to Bury's. Run into the ground by an unscrupulous owner and effectively abandoned by the football authorities, one of whom, the EFL, had been complicit in their decline, they nevertheless refused to give up. Instead, they have created something vibrant from the ashes of their fallen club, a supporter owned option for those who still wanted to follow some incarnation of 'Bury'.

'It's not easy' admits Phil Young, 'and there is a lot of work involved, almost all of it on a voluntary basis. But when you see people at the match and feel that sense of community, you know that it's all worth it.'

EXETER CITY

Exeter City spent most of the 1990s in the financial doldrums, experiencing one period of Administration and losing control of their home, St James Park in the process. On the lookout for a benefactor to take the struggling club off his hands, Exeter chairman, Ivor Doble eventually settled on a consortium headed by two chancers, John Russell and Mike Lewis.

Both men arrived with slightly iffy reputations. Russell, who was appointed chairman, had been the owner of Scarborough FC from 1994 to 2000, presiding over a disastrous period for the club which saw them drop out of league football and amass debts of £1.25m. Lewis (who was appointed vice-chairman at Exeter) had found himself briefly acting as owner of Swansea City during 2001, a tenure described by Lewis himself as 'a complete disaster'.

According to Paul Farley, one-time Trustee with the Exeter City Supporters Trust (ECST), these factors made many fans wary of the new arrivals.

'Despite the promise of new money from Russell

and Lewis, most fans I talked to were canny enough to treat the new owners with caution. Their track record wasn't great and so there was a healthy degree of scepticism around.'

It was a 'healthy degree of scepticism' that had to weather some unusual PR stunts early on in the duo's reign, such as the appointment of Uri Geller as co-chairman [his son was apparently a fan of the club] and the bizarre sight of Michael Jackson visiting the club. In a Geller organised event, Jackson, David Blaine and the soul diva Patti Boulaye made a one-off appearance in Exeter aimed at raising a bit of cash and giving the club's profile a boost (Jackson was even made an honorary director).

'I think a lot of it was a sleight-of-hand' says Farley, 'some smoke and mirrors to distract us from the reality that those two had no money and no idea of how to run a football club.'

Despite claims to the contrary when taking over, it appeared that the duo's business nous and funding were non-existent. Off the pitch, debts rose, bills went unpaid and creditors became restless. On the pitch, form collapsed and the club dropped out of the Football League in 2003.

And then, to cap it all off, in May of the same year, Russell and Lewis were arrested for fraud. It turned out that not only were the pair effectively broke, they were also awarding themselves exorbitant 'consultancy' fees. In 2007, Russell received a 21-month jail sentence for his role in the affair. Lewis was given 200 hours community service after the judge accepted that he had played a lesser part.

With no saviours riding to the rescue and the club on the cusp of extinction, it was left to the ECST, which had been founded in 2000, to ride to the rescue.

Using capital raised from the membership and fundraising amongst the fans, the Trust managed to negotiate a deal to buy a controlling stake (along with responsibility for the club's £4.2m worth of debt) for the price of £20,000.

'And from there, for the first few years, it was just a case of fire-fighting says Paul Farley. 'We were fortunate in being able to broker some favourable deals with players, managers and other clubs, to clear the football debts, which, under UK law, had to be cleared first. After that, we then put the club into a company voluntary arrangement and painstakingly began to work with our creditors to clear the remaining debt. It was an exceptionally tough process but we got there in the end.'

Under the ownership of the ECST, the Grecians were promoted back into the Football League in 2007/8 and have remained there since (even enjoying a few seasons in League One). The club's story since 2003 is one of hope, an illustration of what fan power can achieve and a template of how a football club can be run differently.

'As a club, we are hugely reliant on our fans willing to go that extra yard' says current club chairman, Julian Tagg. 'We have around 3,500 members in the ECST, from which we draw a proportion of our annual budget.

Every year the Trust commits around £100,000 to the club (and sometimes more through sponsorships, gifts and loans). To put this in perspective, this might be the cost of an established centre forward or several first-year professionals.

'The trust also provides much of our volunteer workforce' says Tagg. 'Without these volunteers, who do many important jobs around the stadium, the financial picture would be more challenging.'

Even with the ECST's support, both in terms of manpower and financial support, it's not easy for a club like Exeter to thrive at the level they are at.

'Finances are an issue for all clubs in the Football League. But not having a benefactor makes it even harder for us. And so, we have had to look at the ways that we can do things differently to other clubs, to in effect find a way for us to compete financially while staying true to the Trust model' says Tagg.

One important way that Exeter have done this

has been to invest heavily in their youth set-up. All clubs, to varying degrees, invest in youth, recognising it as a future provider of players there to be potentially sold or used in the main squad. But Exeter have been more successful than most. In recent seasons, the Grecians have earned millions from selling homegrown graduates like Matt Grimes, Ollie Watkins and Ethan Ampadu.

'I could see from the beginning of this project, when the fans first took control, that the future was very much dependent on us bringing youth through. We were never going to have the kind of budget to just spend and spend on players. And so, we've spent a lot, for a club of our size, in this area, investing heavily in the infrastructure we have here.'

When it came to the investment in youth, the club was fortunate in having someone like Tagg as its chairman. He had cut his teeth at Exeter running the club's first-ever U12 team, which then evolved into the current Academy. Tagg, along with Eammon Dolan, played a key role in its development, building a team of twelve boys into an academy of 200.

'With academies, patience is vital' Tagg says. 'It took ten years to get ours into a space where it's functioning to support the club. And then maybe another five or six years to make it how we want it. For us, it is a vital part of our model. We would be in a very different place if it wasn't for our academy.'

Although the club invests heavily in the youth set-up, how Exeter generate income differs little from many other League One and League Two clubs, reliant on a mixture of sponsorship, match day income, and commercial partnerships (with central funding supporting this). But the main difference between Exeter and the overwhelming majority of similar-sized clubs at this level is, like AFC Wimbledon, their aversion to debt.

According to Tagg, Exeter's fan-owned origin story has, to a large extent, shaped this approach. 'I think when you come close to losing your club, which we very nearly did, it makes you slightly risk-averse. The ECST, as the owners, never want the club to end up in that position again. And as chairman, I am ultimately answerable to their wishes in a way that other owners and chairmen are not. At our club, the wishes of the fans, at least expressed via the medium of the ECST, can dictate how the club operates. So, not only has there been a desire to minimise risk, but there has also been a medium to make sure that desire becomes a reality.'

The stability this has created, combined with some savvy decisions off the pitch has enabled Exeter City to claim the title as the Football League's longest-running majority fan-owned club. They might not generate the headlines of AFC Wimbledon, FC United of Manchester or even

Lewes, but quietly, Exeter have been showing their peers that there is a different way of doing football. And that set amidst the financial madness that often characterises football at their level, fan ownership offers a competitive alternative to the norm.

THE FAN LED REVIEW

It's become a popular complaint in the 'Modern Football' era that if more clubs were owned and run like those in the previous chapter, they, and fan power in general, could act as a panacea for all of the game's ills. Many English supporters look jealously across at Germany and pine for a world where the fan is king. They look at the lower ticket prices, the supporter engagement, the sense of a sport that is tethered to reality and wonder why it can't be the same over here?

As the first chapter outlined, the dominance of the private model of ownership in this country is as much cultural as it was a practical response to the problems that the sport presented as it developed in the late nineteenth century. Once established, it then became ubiquitous, reigning unchallenged during the vast majority of the twentieth century. But despite its dominance and its long period of ascendency in the professional game, English football has made significant strides in challenging the primacy of the private model, advancing the cause of supporter ownership during the past thirty years faster than in any other European country.

To go from a position where every professional club was owned privately and supporters had no interest in having a voice to one where several clubs are now community-owned and supporter trusts exist at over 100 clubs across the pyramid, represents a revolution as profound as any that have taken place within the sport's long history.

A plurality of ownership models now exists in the professional and semi-professional game and it is possible for fans, at the majority of levels to consider the possibility that one day, collectively, they could make the transition from the terraces to the boardroom. That represents a seismic shift in fan culture, one that would have been inconceivable just a generation ago.

However, the word to focus on in that paragraph is 'majority'. Although activists at the likes of Liverpool, Manchester United and Chelsea might dream of a future in which the fans one day own the club, it remains a hopelessly unrealistic prospect within the current parameters of the game. Amongst the self-styled 'elite', the sums involved in any takeover are now so large that they are beyond the means of supporter trusts. These clubs are valued in the billions. And although they each boast enough fans to theoretically unite together to afford that, in reality, such a degree of unity and organisation would likely never occur.

This means that the closest such clubs can get to a 'fan-led' takeover, is when wealthy individuals who happen to be supporters, such as the billionaire property developer Nick Candy at Chelsea, try to get involved, which is 'fan led' in name if not in spirit.

But while the financial realities surrounding the 'elite' have long been understood, in recent years this sense of a sport moving beyond the grasp of the supporters has begun to creep further into the game, extending well beyond the confines of the 'Sky Six'.

'As more money has flowed into the higher reaches of football, the cost of buying a club has gone up and up. When a club like Burnley can cost around £170m, you know that we're operating in a world where the idea of fans, through membership subscriptions and passing buckets around on match days, could raise enough cash to fund a buyout are probably gone in the higher reaches. That's not to say that fan activism at that level is pointless. It isn't. We've seen enough recent examples of pressure being brought on clubs to recognise the value of collective action. But, maybe the dream of ownership in the Premier League, for example, is now one that is simply unrealistic in football's current state' says Martin Cloake.

And yet, despite this reality, during the ESL debacle, the idea of greater fan power being introduced across all levels of the game was very much in the air. Barely a day went by without articles appearing in the football media extolling the virtues of the 'German model', its appeal no doubt bolstered by the fact that Bayern Munich and Borussia Dortmund, both of whom were invited to gorge on the financial bounty of the ESL immediately gave it the cold shoulder. Topics such as '50+1' and 'supporter ownership' were regularly trending on social media as a tsunami of angry fans began to question whether, in light of what was proposed, the future of the game could be trusted to private hands.

It was in the wake of the collapse of the ESL, with the fury of the fans still palpable, that the Tory government announced the launch of their long-promised Fan Led Review.

'In some ways' says Richard Irving of the FSA, 'we were fortunate that the ESL furore kicked off when it did. I think the widespread condemnation amongst fans gave the Government the push it needed. It was final proof, if more proof was required, that football was in dire need of reform and in many ways, simply could not be trusted to look after itself any longer.'

The Review, which was launched in the Spring of 2021, involved representatives of over 130 clubs, approximately 21,000 survey responses and the input of numerous football specialists. When it reported in November of that same year it concluded that English football's fragility is the result of three main factors –

- Misaligned incentives to 'chase success'
- Club corporate structures that lack governance, diversity or sufficient scrutiny of decision making by supporters
- The inability of the existing regulatory structure to address the new and complex structural challenges created by the scale of modern professional men's football

To address these problems, it put forward 47 suggestions that if implemented aim to make English football more accountable, diverse and sustainable. From these, ten recommendations were highlighted as being 'key' in any future change to the industry:

1. The creation of an Independent Football Regulator (IREF) who should have a statutory objective of ensuring English football is sustainable and competitive for the benefit of existing and future fans and the local communities football clubs serve.

2. In achieving its objectives, the IREF should utilise a licensing system under which each club operating in professional men's football, i.e Step 5 level (National League) or above would be required to hold a licence to operate, and be subject to various licence conditions.

3. The IREF will operate a system of advocacy to help clubs comply with rules, but also have strong investigatory and enforcement powers.

4. The IREF should have a chair and board with expertise from a range of industries, appointed by a panel of experts separate from the Government. The FA should have observer status on the IREF board.

5. The IREF should publish an annual report setting out its operational and financial performance for the previous year and be accountable to Parliament.

6. The IREF should be set up in a shadow form, working with the industry to ensure it is operationally functional as soon as legislation comes into force.

7. The Government should introduce a financial regulation regime operated by the IREF based on prudential regulation.

8. The IREF should have a proportionality mechanism managing the level of owner subsidies based on the size of a club's existing finances.

9. The Government should explore ways to support the regulation of football agents operating in English football by working with the relevant authorities including FIFA.

10. Through licence conditions, the new 'Owners and Directors Test' should be split into two parts,

one test for owners (i.e. those who own a minimum of 25 per cent shares in the club alone or acting in concert with others) and one test for directors as well as shadow directors, executive management and any individuals holding those roles regardless of job title.

'I think it's probably important to look at the recommendations through the perspective of the super league proposal' says Richard Irving. 'The ESL brought into sharp focus the threats facing the pyramid. Many of the problems affecting the pyramid had of course been around for some time. However, the ESL, with its threat to the very structure of our game, seemed to throw a brighter light on everything. And so, a big part of what the Review was doing was to ensure that the pyramid is protected in the years to come, to make sure that something which we all love so much survives and thrives. The Review wasn't necessarily about revolutionising football, it was about making the existing system work better.'

Football has, of course, been here before. The game has not been without its attempts to reform in the past, many of which failed to introduce meaningful change. There is however a sense that this time it might be different.

'There is unquestionably more political will, both within football and within Government for this moment to actually mean something' thinks

Martin Cloake. 'For example, early on, the EFL made it known that it was open to the idea of an independent regulator, which was a huge development. For the first time, you've got a major football authority effectively saying it can't cope. Allied to that you have a Government that is conscious about appeasing its 'Red Wall' constituencies, places where football really matters. When you're fighting against powerful vested interests, and you saw a taste of that in the negative response to the Review by certain Premier League club executives, it's going to matter that other powerful interests, like the EFL and the Government are on your side.'

The 'taste' that Cloake refers to was seen in the comments issued by both Aston Villa's CEO, Christian Purslow and Crystal Palace's chairman, Steve Parish in response to the report's publication. The former claimed that the IREF could kill the 'golden goose' because of 'over-regulation', while Parish insisted that an IREF would create 'unintended consequences' without indicating what such consequences would be.

Considering the opposition the recommendation will inevitably face, Cloake admits that there is still a long way to go. 'Will all the recommendations be implemented in the way that the Review envisaged? It's probably unlikely. There is going to be a process of negotiation and, inevitably there will be elements of the game that push back against change. And even after what measures do make it come into effect, we will have to remain vigilant. Football is a sport that is riven with vested interests, people who like things the way they are. Getting them to accept lasting fundamental change is going to be a fight.'

Encouragingly, in April of 2022, the Government offered 'formal support' for the Fan Led Review's ten 'key' reconditions. Yet, frustratingly for some, it stopped short of producing a legislative timescale, stating instead that it will publish a white paper in the summer in which the timings and details of its key proposals will be further outlined. This led many activists to worry that the Fan Led Review could end up suffering the same fate as past attempts to reform.

'Every time reform of football has been mooted, the proposals have ended up gathering dust. We need a firm timeline for legislation. And we need it now. This is a once-in-a-generation chance to change football and protect our community clubs' said Niall Couper, CEO of Fair Game.

Despite the recommendations of the report being welcomed by both activists and supporters as a whole, on the issue of fan representation and ownership within football, the Review was less revolutionary than some had hoped. Ideas such as mandated fan directors, giving supporters first refusal on shares when clubs are put up for sale and the creation of a fund to assist trusts in buyouts failed to materialise. Instead, the Fan Led Review merely dipped its toe in the waters of supporter power.

'Of the few ideas put forward to further the power of fans within the game, one of the most interesting related to heritage items' says Joe Blott, chairman of the Liverpool supporter's union, Spirit of Shankly (SOS).

The review recommended that a licence condition of any club that wished to compete in the top six tiers of the pyramid (from the Premier League to Step Two of the National League system) should be the creation, within their articles of association, of a 'Golden Share'. This would require democratic consent to proposed actions relating to identified 'heritage items'. These were proposed to include:

- The sale of the club stadium
- Relocation outside of the local area which is not a temporary part of a redevelopment
- Joining a new competition that is not approved by FIFA, UEFA and the FA and/or leaving a competition in which it currently plays
- Changes to the club badge, first-team home colours, and club playing name

'What you have with this, for the first time', says

Richard Irving, 'is the potential to have legislative underpinning for the importance of "heritage" for fans. That's new. Traditionally, owners have been able to do what they want, to change team colours, to move the stadium wherever they want, to, most importantly in the wake of the ESL, theoretically remove their clubs from certain competitions. In response, fans could protest but ultimately, that's all they could do. With the "Golden Share", in theory, that can only now happen with the consent of the supporters. And this consent will be expressed via a "Community Benefit Society", essentially some kind of fan trust. These are the bodies that the Report mandates will hold the share, placing democratic accountability at the heart of this idea.'

Although the potential blocking of something like the ESL was the headline take from the 'Golden Share' recommendation, the other 'heritage items' remain hugely important. Just ask the Cardiff City fans who have had to endure a change in their club's colours, the Hull City supporters who had to fight against their owner's attempts to change their club's name, or the Everton fans who recently needed to protest against the creation of the ugliest crest in the club's history.

'A kind of owner has emerged in the game in recent decades who treats the emotion surrounding things like a stadium's name or the club's crest as of little consequence. They see football as a business and because businesses rebrand all the time, probably can't understand why fans get so worked up. But as any fan knows, these "heritage items" form an essential part of their club's identity. If this recommendation comes to fruition, then fans will, at last, have some way of fighting back against this trend' says Irving.

Along with the 'Golden Share', the Review also recommended the creation of 'Shadow Boards'. These would be democratically accountable supporter constituted bodies that will work with the existing executive boards. According to the Review, it is envisaged that these boards:

'Be engaged and consulted on (without limitation), the club's strategic vision and objectives; short, medium and long-term business plans, operational matchday issues of concern to supporters, any proposals relating to club heritage items, marketing, merchandising and sponsorship plans, stadium issues and plans, and the club's plan for broader supporter engagement.'

The report also stated that these boards should be seen as a minimum level of consultation, with clubs encouraged to adopt additional mechanisms as appropriate for their circumstances.'

'Although the devil will be in the detail and also how seriously individual clubs take them, we think the 'Shadow Boards' could be a really positive move' says Joe Blott.

In response to the recommendation, the SOS have been one of the most enthusiastic supporters, a perspective no doubt influenced by their pre-existing relationship with Liverpool.

'We already have something similar in existence, so we think this concept could definitely work' Blott explains. 'In the past, we've had calamitous decisions taken by board members based in Boston but the new engagement model we have now established, one underwritten by a legally binding agreement written into the Club's Articles of Association will hopefully prevent that happening again.'

The agreement has seen the creation of a 16-strong Supporters Board led by SOS, who are now legally recognised as Liverpool Football Club's Official Supporters Trust. The SOS have been given ten of the seats available, with the remainder occupied by other supporter bodies, including the Liverpool Disabled Supporters Association, Spion Kop 1906 and the Liverpool Women's Supporters Committee.

But whether, even if created across the game, these boards will really be effective remains uncertain. Not all activists are so sure. There is a fear amongst some, that the 'Shadow Boards' will end up as mere window dressing. One such critic of the idea is Dave

Boyle:

'If this was the late 1990s you might think this is a good idea. It has a very "Blairite", "Football Task Force" feel to it, the idea that if we can all just get together around a big table and thrash things out, everything will be ok. But it's 2021. Things have moved on. Activism has gone beyond mere consultation. We have three decades worth of supporter ownership, of fans actually owning clubs. That's the starting point from which the Review should have gone from, not setting the clock back to 1999.'

According to Boyle, the Shadow Board recommendation is indicative of an approach to football that fundamentally misunderstands the relationship between fan and club

'There is a view that football is just another form of retail. And in retail, the experience of the customer matters to sellers. You have to treat them well, to listen to them otherwise they will go elsewhere. So, from that perspective, something like a "Shadow Board" makes sense. Sellers can get together with customers to understand how to make their retail experience better. But football is not like retail. The customers in this instance do not, in the main, go elsewhere. No matter how badly the club treats them, how poor the football experience is, the "customer" tends to remain loyal. So, with that in mind, there is nothing in this recommendation that will compel clubs to listen to the fans, because, fundamentally, they don't really have to'

Like many other activists involved in the game, Boyle feels that, when it comes to supporter ownership, the Fan Led Review has been something of a missed opportunity.

'I understand why the Review was cautious. There was a sense of "what is possible" and not necessarily "what is needed". And unquestionably, there is a lot of great stuff that has come out of that process. However, the absence of anything really meaningful on supporter ownership, in my opinion, lets the report down. This part of the game has been one of the true success stories in recent decades. And yet it was barely touched. Nobody is saying that you had to necessarily revolutionise the sport. But the Review could've been braver in this area.'

Boyle feels that the process possibly suffered for not having a body like Supporters Direct involved.

'The FSA doubt their brief is wide. Supporters Direct, as it was before the merger, was focused on supporter ownership and enfranchisement. I think, had they still existed in that form then they would have been strongly advocating for the concept of supporter ownership to receive greater consideration during the review. As it was, I think it was only the community business advocate,

Power to Change, who were really pushing for greater advancements in supporter power to take place.'

One of the most innovative ideas put forward by Power to Change was the creation of a £400m Community Club Ownership Trust loan scheme to help supporters' trusts purchase clubs in crisis or when they are put up for sale.

'There are serious barriers to buying football clubs in distress. And that's something that is not always appreciated. The financial implications of a takeover for a trust, in particular, can be significant. We believed that a tie-over fund would solve many of these problems', says Peter Starkings, whose report, *These Clubs Are Ours*, formulated many of the points Power to Change made to the Review.

According to Starkings, this 'up-front capital' could cover the cost of purchase, and the professional fees associated with a buyout (which often put off supporters asked to contribute capital for fan ownership).

'It could also cover initial running costs' he continues. 'For example, debt financing and players' wages for a limited but relatively generous period of time until trusts are in a position to pay back the loan.'

There were several ways that it was envisioned

the Community Club Ownership Trust could be capitalised, including a levy on TV Revenues or a levy raised on the extraordinary profits gambling companies have made from the game since the advent of smartphone-based in-play markets.

'There are ideas out there, like those put forward by Power to Change, that are looking to take the past 30 years of fan activism and supporter ownership onwards to the next level. And yet, we haven't really seen any of that emerge from the Fan Led Review. That side of the game has remained largely untouched. Yes, there are a couple of interesting things in there, like the "Golden Share", but taken as a whole, it's hard not to feel a little short-changed by the recommendations, as good as almost all of them are' says Dave Boyle.

Despite the evident shortcomings of the Fan Led Review, specifically its apparent unwillingness to further expand the cause of supporter ownership, should its recommendations be implemented, even if partially diluted in response to the inevitable opposition they will arouse, it could still represent a step in the right direction, creating a game that is materially better for the fans.

The review was about easing the financial madness, to chase away the unscrupulous owners, to ensure that fans are not faced with clubs selling their stadiums, going into administration or disappearing altogether. For the average punter, happy to pay on the gate and watch the team they love, that is probably enough.

And even for the supporter activists, this would represent a better form of the sport, one where there are fewer flashpoints, where trusts might not have to campaign against owners, where clubs don't face an existential threat that means fans have to step in to save the day.

'Whatever the limitations of the Fan Led Review, at least, right now, we have the possibility of introducing the kind of change that enough people can get behind to make it happen. And, after that, who knows? Maybe this will be the first step on a long-term process of change that one day will include better fan representation?' says Richard Irving.

And, it must be said, that if recommendations like the 'Golden Share' and 'Shadow Boards' work well in practice, then alongside this better run, more sustainable game, fans will have a stronger sense of engagement and inclusion. It's not the same as ownership, but it is better than what existed before. Prior to the Review, the role of supporters within professional football, and the higher reaches of the semi-professional game, was largely one of customers, albeit customers with a pathological sense of brand loyalty. For the first time in the sport's history, should the recommendations come into effect, there will be a regulatory underpinning that outlines the special position of fans within football.

'And that really matters' says Martin Cloake. 'Supporters are, unquestionably more than customers, even though there is a monetary exchange underwriting our relationship with our clubs. The Fan Led Review establishes that fact. For me, and many others involved in fan activism, it brings an end to the decades long debate that has existed regarding what is the role of the 'fan', specifically its "political" dimension. The Review acknowledges that we have a right to hold our clubs to account and that this should form part of the licensing system. Ending that debate gives us a foundation to now build upon. And who knows where we go from here?'

THE FUTURE

There are currently two logics of fandom that the football writer, Alexander Shea believes are at war in the modern game.

'These are those of (1) football as event or carnival, and (2) football as emotional investment. It's a debate that has been defined by French theorists as the clash between plaisir and jouissance' he writes.

Football as 'event', or 'plaisir', is a reference to the kind of support that you'd witness at a World Cup or European Championships. 'In which', he continues, 'fans celebrate each match as some Dionysian event of utopian happiness. Fans, sporting face paint, dancing side by side and doing Mexican waves revel in the now, everyone having a great time. Football becomes a site of consumption: indistinguishable from going to the cinema or a nightclub with the point being to consume "happiness" via beverages, merchandise and gleeful dancing.'

The second model of fandom is that of football as emotional investment. 'Or jouissance' Shea writes. 'The latter loosely translated as taking pleasure from suffering. This is not meant in some sadomasochistic, Nietzschean sense, but rather in a more quotidian context. We "get off" on suffering a little bit; it is the reason why cyclists both relish and dread the uphill climb.'

The model that underpinned the ESL, with its focus not only on elite clubs and superstar players but also the removal of relegation - and all the associated psychological horrors it brings - was rooted in 'plaisir'. This was football as spectacle, an 'event' experience geared not just towards fans, but also towards neutrals and those who wear their colours lightly. This was not Burnley and West Brom grinding out a 0-0.

'Make no mistake, the people who run elite clubs are eager to move away from what the ESL derisively dismissed as "Legacy" fans, the kind who have been following clubs for years, who live and die for them and who probably still miss the pre-Premier League football world. The elite clubs are instead focused on corporate clientele, tourists and, perhaps most important of all, the TV revenue that can be generated from fans and 'neutrals' in emerging markets. They are chasing a different kind of "football customer" - to use their language' says Martin Cloake.

For those of us of a certain age, likely those who lived through the pre-1992 world, the notion of what constitutes a 'fan' can sometimes be a little ridged. It is often defined as someone who physically goes to the game and who is emotionally invested, to a deep degree, in what is occurring on the pitch. It is also somebody who only follows that club and who does so for life.

But changes taking place within the sport and within fans themselves suggest that this perspective is woefully narrow. Recent research has revealed that, although still small, an increasing number of younger fans, those drawn from the 16-24 age bracket, are not just more likely to switch clubs season-to-season in search of success, but are also able to hold multiple allegiances.

Before the start of the 2015/16 season, a survey undertaken by the Premier League into fandom amongst the young found that one in ten fans were going to change their allegiances to a new team before a ball had been kicked, with the then champions, Chelsea, being the main beneficiary. Although still a small minority, the fact that the ultimate footballing taboo no longer carries the stigma it once did shows the instability of the foundations upon which the 'traditional' definition of 'fandom' are built.

This is further illustrated by a recent study undertaken by Copa90 which revealed that an incredible 27 per cent of young fans (within the 16-24 age bracket) now support three or more teams. While this trend towards plurality often includes teams from the non-league world, there is also a tendency for supporters to be international in their reach, with fans of Premier League clubs embracing an affiliation with members of the continental European elite, most notably Barcelona and Real Madrid.

To complement these changes, some young fans are also beginning to follow players rather than just clubs. Copa90 found that for those in that same age bracket, player brands and their social media profiles play a significant role in how they now interact with the game. You saw a hint of this when Ronaldo moved to Juventus from Real Madrid in 2018. In the aftermath of the transfer, Real lost one million Twitter followers within 24 hours. Conversely, the Serie A club gained 3.5 million Instagram followers, 1.7 new Facebook followers, 350,000 new Twitter followers and 500,000 new YouTube subscribers.

These shifting foundations of what constitutes a 'fan' are occurring at the same time as a change in the nature of football 'consumption' is taking place. The Premier League and the Champions League have become entertainment products, beamed around the world to people in their millions. In 2019/20 the cumulative global viewership of the Premier League, for example, was 3.2bn people. In total, 190 countries now receive the English top-flight, and in many of these countries, such as

Egypt and India, our elite division is now more watched than their own. The Premier League has become the most-watched football league worldwide, accounting for 42 of the top 50 global audiences for European domestic league matches and recording the largest audiences in China, India and the USA.

And what does this audience want? Judging by the staggering followings that top sides now boast and the fact that fixtures featuring elite teams regularly top the viewing charts, it's not a relegation dog fight between two struggling 'minnows'. The TV market, which has become the most important element of 'fan-led' income within the game is routinely focused on those competing at the top of the pyramid. Even those neutrals who don't have a horse in the race would rather, it seems, sit through games featuring the likes of Liverpool, Chelsea and Manchester City than sides such as, Norwich City, Southampton and Crystal Palace.

And, if the UK is anything to go by, this TV audience also doesn't want uncertainty, at least according to a paper published in the International Journal of Economics of Business a few years ago. As the report's authors wrote:

'The classic notion of a pure sporting contest in which the outcome is unpredictable has been replaced with one in which the preference is for sporting entertainment delivered by superstars'

Adherents of the game have long believed that the notion that 'anyone can beat anyone' was essential to the popularity of football. And yet, amongst some who now consume the sport that is evidently not the case. They don't want Aston Villa to beat Liverpool, Crystal Palace to vanquish Manchester City, Brentford to defeat Chelsea. They crave predictability instead, which is possibly why a league whose higher reaches have become increasingly staid in recent decades still remains so immensely popular.

For these consumers, the need for excitement that unpredictability once provided is satisfied in other ways. The reports' authors suggested that it can come instead from the reflected 'glamour' of elite fixtures and in big name players strutting their stuff. The prospect of watching Ben Mee and James Tarkowski cannot compare, it appears, to the allure of Mo Salah, Bruno Fernandes and Kevin De Bruyne.

It's also arguable that the game has augmented itself to keep this audience entertained by creating more 'excitement' in an average match. Specifically, you can see this in attempts to increase the number of goals per game. So, not only does English football, for example, now have a monied elite that can assemble squads capable of decimating less financially endowed clubs, but the rules have also been altered to ensure that goals flow more easily too, such as changes to the backpass law, the judgement of offside, and the way in which referees interpret contact - all of which have gradually given forwards more protection and greater opportunities to score.

You also see this desire for more goals expressed in the language used and the narrative's woven by the sport's broadcasters. It's there in the dismissal of so called 'anti-football', in the loaded comments of 'only one team wanted to play football today', in the praise doled out to clubs like Leeds and Fulham but not to the likes of Burnley or Watford. In the media narrative, these latter types, teams that refuse to play all-out, gung-ho football, who restrict not just their own opportunities to score but also the opposition's, are failing to contribute to the 'entertainment'. They are letting the side down and so are publicly denigrated for making choices that, if 'entertainment' is taken out of the equation, represent perfectly valid tactical decisions.

Football is now akin to the film industry. And what those responsible for running and televising the game want is blockbusters; big, spectacular, easy to digest visual events, which in the absence of a deep emotional pull, will keep that ever-expanding armchair audience engaged. In place of Hollywood royalty, Sky serve up Sadio Mane, Cristiano Ronaldo and Harry Kane, recognisable stars to pull you in. And then, when they've got you, 'goals' play the part of the heavily choreographed fight scene, the ten-minute car chase, the giant motion-captured Andy Serkis gorilla. They are there to stop your attention wavering, to sate your need for easy gratification.

What people like UEFA and the Premier League don't want is a low-budget, Guardian acclaimed, indie film. The kind that might be in a foreign language and deal with complex emotional and social issues, like a film about Syrian refugees or family breakdown in rural Croatia starring Craig Cathcart. For them, that's what a tightly fought, relatively incident-free 0-0 between two 'minnows' is. It might be well crafted, riven with subtext and expertly put together, but it's not something that they think the average punter wants to watch.

And, considering the shifts that are taking place within fandom and football 'consumption', they might have a point.

In light of these changes, if you were to put yourself into the shoes of an elite club owner, like one of the Glazers or John Henry (just try to supress your conscience for a minute), then you can appreciate why efforts to move football in the direction of something like the ESL are taking place. Aside from the huge financial windfall member clubs would accrue, there is a sense that such a breakaway league is responding to alterations within the game that are already taking place. They are alterations that are creating a potential future in which the idea of elite clubs, boasting recognisable stars, playing each other regularly for a mass TV market, with membership of this market fairly guaranteed, does not seem so outlandish. It's not inconceivable to envisage a time when some kind of breakaway league, filled with elite teams and superstar players and with the prospect of relegation removed, would have an audience. That's not to say that it would be universally loved but rather that enough people would exist to make it viable.

Already, we have a quasi-version of this in the Champions League, a competition whose founding concept was rooted in elitism. In the old European Cup, where only actual champions were permitted to compete, the unpredictability of the knockout system meant that 'smaller' clubs from 'peripheral' football nations could, if luck was on their side, make it to the closing stages. But that is less common in the modern version of Europe's elite competition. Now, the lengthy qualification process, the grinding group stage and a seeding system that benefits the elite ensure that the latter stages are roughly populated by the same handful of clubs and faces each year. What's more, with every reform made to the competition, such as recent attempts to award places to clubs based on 'legacy' status rather than just sporting merit, UEFA illustrate their long-held desire to turn the Champions League into an effective closed shop.

And yet, regardless of this blatant elitism, it is also a competition that remains immensely popular. The final is the world's most-watched annual sporting event, aired in more than 200 countries and with an estimated global average audience in the region of 165m. It seems that regardless of its pervasive sense of sterility, all people really want is 'sexy' footballers, big teams and relative predictability.

But, despite the changes taking place within football fandom and football consumption, specifically amongst younger fans, the days of the "traditional" supporter, as embodied in the "Legacy Fan" are far from numbered. The scale of the uproar that greeted the ESL revealed that. The widescale disapproval amongst supporters, irrespective of where their club stood on the football pyramid, was telling. It illustrated that the hopes amongst elite owners that the creation of a sport peopled by happy-clapping, smiling fans and neutrals watching fixtures for the spectacle alone, free from those bothersome emotional connections that prevent "Legacy" fans from enjoying anything as anodyne as the ESL is still out of reach. At least for now.

The truth is that although the game increasingly wants to treat fans like customers, for many people football remains a very different animal. There is a visceral connection to clubs that cannot be explained away by market economics. On cold, hard analysis, there is no reason, for example, for anyone in their right mind to support a club like Everton. The club regularly tops the polls as one of the most depressing to support in England. Decades of mediocrity, frustration and the sense of aimless drift have gradually robbed any joy that can be derived from following the Toffees. And so, logically, considering what is available just across Stanley Park, it would make more sense, in pure economic terms, if the time and money spent on Everton was instead invested in Liverpool. Yet, no Evertonian in their right mind would do this. And that's because, despite the changes that are taking place within the game, if football fans do have a sense of brand loyalty, for many it is one so loyal, so unwavering and so hard to fathom that it should probably come with a mental health warning. It would be like choosing to continually shop in Tesco after enduring repeated bouts of food poisoning from their products, even though a perfectly good Asda is just down the road.

The politicisation of football supporters over the past thirty years, in many ways, represents a deepening of this unwavering loyalty. If fans really were just customers, then clubs like AFC Wimbledon, Clapton CFC and FC United of Manchester would not exist. Equally, clubs like Exeter City, Portsmouth and Swansea City would have long gone out of business. Faced with a game that is changing at a rapid pace and often beyond recognition, supporters at all levels of the game have fought back.

The Fan Led Review, despite its limitations, appears to accept this. Through recommendations like the 'Golden Share' and the 'Shadow Boards', along with the desire to create a sport more tethered to economic sanity and one which recognises the importance of football clubs to local communities, the Review is probably the boldest statement yet to outline the concept of supporters being more than customers.

Whether every recommendation will become reality only time will tell. Football has been run in a certain way for a very long time and those who have done well from it will likely not take kindly to being told that things should be run differently. As the ESL debacle revealed, some of the most powerful figures in the English game have a view on the future of football that is almost diametrically opposed to the future envisaged by many supporter activists. Reconciling these differing perspectives will not be easy.

And so, the question arises, where does supporter ownership fit into this shifting landscape?

'Fan ownership and supporter activism, in general, has come a long way from its beginnings in the late-1980s. In fact, fans in this country have probably taken a bigger journey than any others in Europe. Back in the 1980s, the idea of having supporter-owned clubs in England, as you had in Germany and Spain, would have seemed really unrealistic. So, that shift needs to be appreciated. Not only do we now have several fan-owned clubs, but we also have the sense of "politicisation" amongst supporters that can be seen in club level campaigns and in wider, cross-club movements, such as Fans Supporting Foodbanks.' says Dave Boyle.

But, despite these achievements, Boyle feels that there are still limitations constraining the movement:

'Most importantly, there is no will amongst football authorities to change the game. Within football, at the FA, the Premier League, the EFL and even in the National League, there appears little appetite for greater fan control. Although these bodies could, in theory, intervene to support the model, none have ever declared a desire to do so. They aren't necessarily hostile to supporter ownership, they just don't really care one way or the other.'

Part of the problem, thinks Boyle, lies in the fact that football, as it currently stands, mostly works.

'Yes, there are problems and yes, it is far from perfect. However, it still basically functions and, in the main, most fans appear happy with that. The game has yet to reach a crisis point whereby some revolution in ownership becomes imperative. And, if the recommendations of the Fan Led Review are implemented, creating a better functioning game, nor is this likely in the immediate future.'

Beyond football, in the world of politics, this indifference to fan ownership continues. At the moment, none of the main political parties appear to value the meaningful extended reach of fans into the game. For the Tories, the kind of Government intervention required to restructure football along democratic lines is something that clashes violently with their 'hand-off', market-friendly, pro-business ideology. The same is largely true of Labour, specifically in their current 'Blairite' guise. Although noises within the party have been made in the recent past about extending fan ownership, these noises have been much quieter since the demise of the Corbyn experiment. By its very nature, extending supporter control via legislation means tackling the primacy of the private business model. The current Labour party are far too wary of frightening the middle ground to attempt anything so remotely 'socialist'.

But, argues Boyle, the factors limiting the movement actually go beyond the attitude of the Government and the football authorities. There are also the limited horizons of the fans themselves to consider.

'Most fan campaigns, and specifically those that have led to a takeover, have tended to be reactive. That is to say, they respond to a crisis rather than setting the pace themselves. With supporter ownership, it's clear that fans tend to only take up the reigns in response to a crisis, whether that be a financial one, such as what happened at Exeter City and Lewes, or a crisis of frustration, as in the example of FC United of Manchester. Clubs are not being taken over spontaneously or founded because supporters think they have a right to own their clubs.'

Fans become, in effect, owners of last resort, there to ride to the rescue when other options have run out. Whether it is Exeter City on the brink of ruin, AFC Wimbledon following the original club's desertion to Milton Keynes or Clapton FC disenfranchising the fans, supporter power has long been a reactive force.

'Although you do have an "activist" element at clubs, the kind of people who are always seeking to hold the board to account, the truth is that when things are going well, most fans are happy to let the club get on with running things. Most people just want to watch football and see their team finish as high as possible. That doesn't mean they love it any less than the "activist". It just means they don't see their involvement in the game as having a "political" dimension. That could easily change if suddenly the club was faced with going into Administration or the owner was doing terrible things to it. But, under normal circumstances, when things are going well, or even just alright, most fans are happy to just be football fans' says Richard Irving.

In England, we regularly see private individuals take over football clubs that aren't in crisis. And yet, historically, the same has not been true of the fans. The supporter trust movement has lacked an assertive character. Although almost all of its member organisations have 'club ownership' as their stated intent, attempting to implement this aim in any meaningful way in the absence of a catastrophic opportunity presenting itself, has not been the norm.

'Without a crisis, you tend to not have the numbers, the finance or motivation amongst enough people. Although lots of fans might sympathise with a trust's aims, that doesn't mean they're going to do anything about it. In reality, a crisis is a great motivator. Good times, or even average times, are not. We've come a long way in this country when it comes to activism. But there is still a long way to go. For the movement to become more meaningful probably requires a culture change, one that would see fans start to think "why not us?" when it came to ownership, whatever is happening at their club' says Andy Walsh.

This sense of fans focusing on what occurs on the pitch, which is after all the reason why we fall in love with football in the first place, also has ramifications for the sustainability of fan ownership at those clubs who have adopted this model.

'The problem with being fan-owned is that remaining competitive is a challenge' says Ivor Heller. 'A club like ours, which differs little to other supporter-owned clubs, has the money it makes from the ground, match-day revenue, sponsorship, commercial arrangements, broadcast deals and the investment it gets from the trust. There is no sugar daddy offering soft loans to let us spend freely. We are run sustainably and we don't go into debt. But we're competing with teams that do have a benefactor to turn to and who do spend freely and go into debt. So, inevitably, competing is hard.'

This creates a situation in which fans at supporter-owned clubs might have to accept a possible cap on their aspirations. Or, in more extreme circumstances, the reality of football at a much lower level, as Donald Kerr, current vice-chairman of Brentford and until recently, secretary of the club's supporters trust, explains:

'As a fan, you want to watch good football and feel that your team has a chance of doing well. When the trust, Bees United, was in charge at Brentford this simply wasn't the case. If anything, the club seemed more likely to drop down into the Conference. The budget we had was unsustainable for League football. We were conscious, because we are fans too, that in time, this would prove unpopular and there might be a moment when the fans turned on the trust. This was part of the reason why we looked for a new investor. We were very careful how we did this and made sure we passed ownership to a genuine fan, Matthew Benham, who clearly had the funds and vision to take the club forward. If we hadn't taken this path then I'm confident that, under the fans, the club would have just deteriorated on the pitch.'

In the immediate aftermath of a crisis, when the trust has stepped in and taken control, there tends to be a lot of goodwill floating around towards the new fan-owners. Not only have they usually saved the club from oblivion but their ranks are made up of people with whom the rest of the wider fanbase can have an affinity.

'And that's great because often, in the early days, life is tough. At Exeter, the trust's early years in charge were mostly spent fire-fighting, dealing with the financial calamity created by the former owners. But over time, there is a danger that memory of the crisis fades and with that, the goodwill ebbs too. And, added to that, you'll always have younger fans coming through who have no first-hand memory of the crisis and who might wonder why the trust needs to be in charge. The problem then is that if you're not doing well on the pitch, possibly because of the financial limitations of the trust model, then supporters are going to start thinking that maybe it's time to try something else' says Julian Tagg.

Supporter ownership can come into conflict with the very essence of what makes a fan a fan. Clubs run in this fashion are sometimes asking supporters to potentially trade success on the pitch for stability and sustainability off it. And while there will always be some fans who are willing to do that, likely those who are more politically aligned with the concept of democratic control, there will always be those who won't. If football is about anything, then it is about upward progression. When we align with a club at a young age we want them to win and to finish as high as possible in the pyramid. As kids, we don't fall in love with a club because we want them to be community-owned and run in a sustainable and stable fashion.

Not that the promise of 'stability' always come to fruition. Although most fan-owned clubs have delivered on that front, there have been those who have failed. Sadly, for advocates of supporter ownership, the model does not necessarily guarantee that the right people end up running a club. Supporters are still people, and people are more than capable of falling short, as the case of

Stockport County revealed a few years ago.

Back in 2005, the Stockport County Supporters Trust (SCST) took control of the club for a nominal fee of £1. They bought it off departing owner, Brian Kennedy, whose company, Cheshire Sports had been running County, at a significant loss, since 2003.

Although the deal contained several positive elements, such as a six-year sponsorship agreement with Cheshire Sport, which amounted to around £750,000, and a 25-year, rent-free lease of the club's ground, Edgeley Park, some other parts were less beneficial to Stockport's future. Key amongst these was a stipulation that Cheshire Sports would take a majority share of match-day revenue and a 30 per cent cut of all transfer fees.

A loss-making business saddled with a deal that siphoned off a significant part of its revenues made life difficult for the trust-owned club. Under the control of the supporters, the financial situation worsened considerably and in the spring of 2009, County were eventually forced into Administration. At the time the club owed over £7m. The accountancy firm Leonard Curtis was appointed Administrators and the all-too-common search for a saviour began, one that pointedly was not going to see the 'fans' as part of any solution.

When flattering articles about supporter

ownership appear in the press, journalists tend to highlight the success stories, the likes of AFC Wimbledon, FC United of Manchester and Exeter City. And yet, the instances where things don't go well, like Stockport County, are just as important. Running a football club is not easy and these ventures can fall foul to the same forces that have been picking apart the dreams of club owners since the dawn of the professional game: over-reach, incompetence and bad luck.

It's perhaps the existence of these 'failures', combined with the financial, organisational and administrative challenges that ownership represents that has left supporters reluctant to see themselves as anything other than owners of last resort. No fan wants to be part of the trust that takes a perfectly fine football club and runs it into the ground.

And yet, maybe that desire to take a risk, to grab control of the reins even if things aren't that bad, is about to change? At least if the case of Dunstable Town is anything to go by.

The Bedfordshire club have had a long and mixed history. Formed in 1883 they've folded twice, had the likes of George Best and Jeff Astle in their ranks, and had the dubious honour of once being managed by Barry Fry. Currently in their third iteration, the Blues have flitted from the Spartan South Midland League to the Southern Premier over the last decade or so. Essentially, a resolutely Step 5/6 club.

'A few years ago, our club had already transitioned into a kind of supporter-owned model when we had reverted to a members' club after our previous chairman decided to leave' says current club chairman, Andrew Madaras.

The chairman had initially proposed handing the club over to a local consortium whose ideas for the immediate future for the side had gone down very badly with the supporters.

'Their plan was for our club to take a voluntary relegation down three divisions. They thought that the income of the club was more suited to the lower levels of the National League system. Although they possibly had a point, we are, after all, not a club that generates a lot of revenue, for a lot of us it felt like a bit of a capitulation. So, in response, around twenty to thirty of us bandied together to become members and take over the club' says Madaras.

It's a type of ownership not uncommon to the nether regions of the non-league world, where clubs frequently still adhere to the membership model pioneered during the Victorian football boom. But ironically, despite adopting this model principally to resist the 'relegation' plans of the consortium, the club went on to endure successive relegations in the two seasons that followed.

'A lot of clubs at our level find life incredibly difficult' says Madaras. 'We are not helped by the fact that we don't own our stadium and therefore find it hard to maximise our revenue. However, we're not alone in this. Life is tough in the lower reaches of the pyramid. And with the budget we had, we just struggled. And then Covid arrived, which just made everything that bit harder.'

Like a lot of non-league clubs, Dunstable Town rely on FA prize money and local sponsorship for a big part of their revenue, two factors that were hit by the pandemic.

'With prize money halved by the FA and local businesses tightening their belt in response to the economic problems created by Covid, a lot of clubs at our level were finding life a challenge. We were no exception. The routine struggles of life in the lower reaches of the national league system just became that much harder. And like other clubs that do not have a benefactor to turn to, you have to start thinking creatively about how you fund the club going forward. And it was while thinking about what we could do that the example of Lewes kept coming to mind' Madaras recalls.

Having visited the Dripping Pan, talked to the chairman and directors and read about the club, he had been impressed by what the Sussex club was doing; its community work, the progressive move on gender equality and, most importantly, its ownership structure.

'I just felt that they were showing that there was a different way of doing football. It was as though moving to supporter ownership had unleashed this tremendous creative force at the club and energised the place. I felt that a move to that model might benefit us too. Not only could it represent another, hopefully, more sustainable stream of income, but I was also hoping it could enable us to engage better with the community and energise our club too.'

After discussions with the membership, the decision was taken to approach the FSA about exploring the possibility of transitioning the club's existing model into community ownership. Dunstable eventually made the move in 2021.

'This was a really positive development', says Richard Irving. 'Dunstable Town were something different. Although the club was not exactly having the best time financially, there was no severe, life-threatening crisis or the sense that the fans were in open revolt. Instead, this was a fairly average non-league side, deciding that fan ownership was the way to go. I think it represented a hugely important moment for the model. For some time, this is what we have been pushing for.'

In some ways, the example of Dunstable Town has

a similar feel to the hoped-for potential impact that Portsmouth's conversion to supporter ownership promised back in 2014. Back then, Pompey's embracing of the model suggested that a new phase in the movement's future beckoned; that 'Punk Football', and specifically majority ownership by the fans, was poised to reach further into the game, to move from being something that only functioned in the lower regions of the Football League and below to something that represented a possible way of doing football in the Championship and above.

Of course, Portsmouth's impact proved to be negligible. The reality of life under fan ownership proved too restrictive for a set of fans, understandably accustomed to the better things in life.

Will Dunstable Town's potential also prove just as illusory? Only time will tell. Certainly, their decision to move into fan ownership represents an acknowledgement, for the first time that putting the fans in control is potentially an option irrespective of what condition a club is in. It's a shift that if replicated could have a profound impact on the number of fan-owned clubs that might populate English football in the years to come.

At the moment, beyond legislation, supporter ownership remains limited by finance and mentality. The former will remain a problem. It's the reason why we are unlikely to see a fan-owned club in the Championship or the Premier League. And it's a big reason why many fans remain wary of ownership. It costs a lot to take over most clubs. Even those in the National League system don't come cheap, because although the price is lower, so too is the purchasing power of the collective fanbase.

But, as Dave Boyle argues, 'mentality' plays a role too, the belief that fans not only can do this but they have an equal right to. English football has been run and owned in a very specific way for a very long time, so, understandably, the challenge to the primacy of the private owner has only happened slowly. The stereotypical image of the 'local-boy-made-good' seated at the head of the board is so ingrained within the popular consciousness that it was always going to take some shifting.

Not least because, giving in to that reality is so much easier. Being a fan-owned club is hard. It takes work, it takes sacrifice and it includes the possibility that success on the pitch might be harder to come by. By contrast, throwing your club open to some deep-pocketed benefactor is so much easier. Although it might come with risks, it takes almost no work and arrives with the tantalising possibility of instant success.

Set against this, and the sheer weight that 'tradition' can bring - the sense that this is how something has always been, so why change things - reframing the consciousness of football supporters to believe that the right to own their club is something that exists at all times and not just when a club is facing material danger, has not been straightforward. It's taken thirty years of functioning examples of fan ownership combined with the near-endless stream of failed clubs and dodgy owners to erode the dominance that the 'traditional' model of ownership long held in the popular consciousness.

And, even now, it is just one set of fans at one club that have taken this bold step. But, as with any revolution, it has to start somewhere. Back in 1992, supporter ownership was just a few fans owning a minority share at Northampton Town. It's taken time but from those inauspicious beginnings, a movement has grown that continues to leave its mark on the game.

If Dunstable Town were to thrive under their new owners, in thirty years we could be looking back at the club in the same way that we look back at Northampton Town from the vantage point of today, as pioneers for a different way of doing football.

And there is little doubt that what Dunstable are doing could be replicated elsewhere. While, inevitably, much of the focus on the suitability of fan ownership in the modern game is focused on its feasibility, or lack of it, at the top, for great swathes of the game supporter control remains tantalisingly within reach. For those competing in the National League system and below, fan ownership is a perfectly viable alternative to the traditional model. And even upwards, into the lower levels of the Football League, it can still deliver a competitive option.

Importantly, it can do this at any time. Should fans, collectively, be able to organise a takeover, there is no reason why a trust should have to wait for some kind of existential crisis before making their move. As long as the financial sums make sense, then there is nothing preventing a trust, or any other form of fan group, from believing that it has the right to consider a takeover or a transition into fan control, even in happier times.

Despite the hiccups, the false dawns and the frustrated aspirations, the history of the punk football movement during the past 30 years is one of undeniable success. Success in saving clubs, success in creating clubs. But more than anything 'success' in establishing the viability of the model. There now exists a functioning, tried and tested alternative to the traditional style of ownership in this country. And it is one that is applicable to almost any group of supporters. But it's extension into the game will likely never be handed down from above. Instead, it will need to be something that emerges from the grassroots, from pioneers like Dunstable Town, those fans amongst us who when pondering the question, 'who should run this club?', don't see any reason why the answer can't be 'Me'.

BOOKS BY THIS AUTHOR

Is It Just Me Or Is Modern Football S**T?: An Encyclopaedia Of Everything That Is Wrong In The Modern Game

Does the sight of half-scarves enrage you? Does transfer-deadline day make you want to throw a brick through the TV? Do the opening bars of goal music make your ears bleed? If the answer is 'yes', then this could be the book for you. Since English football's very own 'Year Zero' in 1992, the game has changed beyond recognition, rejecting the rough-and-ready days of the past. And like any change, not all of it has been welcome. The quality of the 'football product' might be better but it's come with spiralling levels of debt, yawning inequality and Neymar advertising batteries. These, and many other ills of the modern game, form Jim Keoghan's exploration of the nation's favourite pastime. Navigating a world populated by dodgy owners, celebrity referees and

Ray Winstone's floating head, he searches for an answer to the question: Is it Just Me or is Modern Football S**t?

BOOKS BY THIS AUTHOR

How To Run A Football Club: The Story Of Our National Game

How to Run a Football Club is the story of our national game. Told through a journey up the pyramid, from the muddy pitches and ramshackle changing rooms at grass-roots level to the glitz and glamour of the Premier League, the book explores that common theme that links the game at all levels - the simple love of the sport. It's there in the volunteer coaches who give up their Saturday mornings to teach kids how to play, the non-league club secretaries trying their best to get the pitch in good shape and the owners and investors risking their wealth in the unpredictable world of English football. How to Run a Football Club delves into their stories to find out what motivates the people who keep the game alive. It explores how the sport is evolving, with the growth of women's football, walking football and esports. What does it take to run a good football club? How is money, or a lack of it, changing the game? Read this book to find out.

BOOKS BY THIS AUTHOR

Punk Football: The Rise Of Fan Ownership In English Football

Punk Football tells the story of how supporters have made the incredible journey from the terraces to the boardroom. Initially intrigued by the rise of AFC Wimbledon, the supporter-owned club set up after Wimbledon FC's relocation to Milton Keynes, Jim Keoghan was drawn into a world in which ordinary fans have started new clubs, taken a stake in those they once followed and sometimes saved clubs from disappearing altogether. The fan-ownership movement has touched every echelon of the game, challenging the private model that has dominated football for over a century. There have been highs and lows, successes and failures, but through it all the dogged determination of fans to be more than paying customers has shone through. Regarded as a revolutionary force in modern sport, the story of Punk Football is one that will appeal to every fan who has ever thought, "I could run this club better myself."

Printed in Great Britain
by Amazon